Praise for *S.K.I.R.T.S. in the Boardroom*

"Marshawn has developed a solid formula to inspire and empower today's working women. This book gives women of all backgrounds the tools not only to succeed but also to become leaders in their workspace."

—Michelle Lemmons, Founder and Chairman,
International Speakers Bureau

"A must-have survival guide for women in any male-dominated industry who are trying to break through the glass ceiling. I've worked in the finance and sports industries for many years and only wish I'd had access to this book when I began my career. Now that I do, I'm never putting it down!"

—Rama Mandadi, Senior Manager, National Basketball Association

"Marshawn Evans knows how to dream big dreams and persevere in the face of an uphill battle. She knows how to learn the lessons offered by disappointing setbacks, naysayers, and obstacles that seem as permanent as a brick wall. In this book, she pours out what she has learned in a way that is approachable and friendly."

—Valorie Burton, Life Coach and author of *Why Not You?*

"*S.K.I.R.T.S. in the Boardroom* is powerful, straightforward, and a must read for all women. It addresses the core of what most women want, and it shows them *how* to realize their dreams without fear or compromise. Through Marshawn's own experience and intellect, she shares how being mentally tough, spiritually centered, and properly prepared is a powerful combination in any boardroom! This book *will* make a difference!"

—Gwen Wilson, Director of Women's Business Initiatives
and Supplier Diversity, Verizon Wireless

"Marshawn just may well be the next Oprah! Her natural business sense and ideas address winning solutions for today's marketplace. Her ability to design, develop, and deliver critical business solutions puts her in a unique class of entrepreneurs. Definitely a woman to watch!"

—Kenton Clarke, President and CEO, DiversityBusiness.com

"Being a professional woman in a male-dominated industry is not easy. Marshawn has been there and offers real-world strategies for rising women looking to embrace femininity in a world of uncharted territory. She shows women how to break through the glass ceiling with panache and in a killer pair of pumps!"

—E. Monique Johnson, Managing Editor of *Upscale Magazine*

"With clarity, humor, and insight, Marshawn uses analogies relatable to all women. Whether a CEO of a major Fortune 500 company or a mother of four who has chosen to stay at home, we can all identify with the principles Marshawn so eloquently delivers. Whatever our life's path, success is truly a state of mind."

—Kaye Burkhardt, President, Dallas Fan Fares, Inc.

"*S.K.I.R.T.S. in the Boardroom* provides insightful, empowering guidance for women, for use in the business world and everywhere else! Marshawn Evans draws on a wide range of personal experiences to deliver compelling, relevant advice in a relatable way, complete with frankness and humor. No matter what stage of your career, you will glean new insights and will also be reminded of things you already know, but just don't do often enough. A great addition to your personal library!"

—Kellie Appel, Senior Vice President, *Broadcasting*

"Wow! I simply love this book. I couldn't put it down once I started it. Seldom does a book say it better or more powerfully than *S.K.I.R.T.S. in the Boardroom*. This book is a must read for those who want to navigate the slippery slope of climbing the ladder of success in business and life. My heartfelt thanks go out to Marshawn Evans for giving us this important gem."

—George Fraser, author of *Click* and *Success Runs in Our Race*

"Lose your stereotypes about beauty pageant stars. Marshawn Evans' brains can cash the checks her publicity is writing."

—TDJakes.com

"Marshawn Evans is a marketing wizard with a love for living on the edge. She shows others how to create a fantastic future!"

—Amira Kidd, *Monarch Magazine*

"Marshawn has gone from problem child to one of the top women in America. Her savvy business brawn is simply inspiring. She loves to get up in the morning, and I can see why."

—Vince Poscente, author of *The Age of Speed*

"Marshawn is far and away the best black female candidate to ever compete for Trump's apprenticeship."

—Alfred Edmond, Editor-in-Chief of *Black Enterprise* magazine

S·K·I·R·T·S·
IN THE BOARDROOM

A Woman's Survival Guide to Success in Business & Life

MARSHAWN EVANS, JD

WILEY

John Wiley & Sons, Inc.

For general information on our other products and services or for technical support, please contact our Customer Care Department within the United States at (800) 762-2974, outside the United States at (317) 572-3993 or fax (317) 572-4002.

Wiley also publishes its books in a variety of electronic formats. Some content that appears in print may not be available in electronic books. For more information about Wiley products, visit our web site at www.wiley.com.

ISBN: 978-0-470-38333-9

Printed in the United States of America
10 9 8 7 6 5 4 3 2 1

To my grandmothers—
Lendell Evans and Pearline Veal
—the original S.K.I.R.T.S.

A Brief Excerpt from *S.K.I.R.T.S. in the Boardroom*

For many of us, listening to ourselves is a skill to be learned rather than a habit we have already acquired. This is due to environment. In the hurly-burly world of high-stakes, fast-paced business dealings, it can often feel as if you need to talk twice as fast just to keep up. Unfortunately, when the workday is done, we are still operating in catch-up mode and think that listening to ourselves is a luxury, not a necessity. But, as in most things, it is quality, not quantity, that counts when it comes to listening—particularly when it comes to listening to your own inner voice.

As Albert Einstein once said, "The monotony and solitude of a quiet life stimulates the creative mind." Think about it. Where do you have your best ideas and most inspiring thoughts? In the shower? In the bathroom? (Don't be embarrassed—it's just girl talk!) If you are a driven woman with big dreams, the challenge for you is the same challenge I deal with everyday—taking quality "me" time. I was in law school at Georgetown when I bought my first home in Atlanta. At age 25, I was extremely excited to become a homeowner after 20 years of schooling (starting with kindergarten). One of the big selling points was the huge bathtub in the master bedroom. So, I moved into the house. Two years passed by, and guess what? I used the bathtub only two times in two years! Instead, I would always choose to use the shower. It was, and still is, the quickest option. With a shower, I have instant water and maybe eight seconds to wait before the water is hot and ready for business! However, my bathtub is on the third floor, so I have to wait longer for the water to get hot, and then I have wait for the tub to fill up. It is a longer wait, which requires more patience and preplanning. I have to budget my time better to allow for the water to heat up and fill up. But I made a resolution to myself to use that time as "me" time. And, it has been worth it. I actually had a revelation one day. The word B.A.T.H. is an acronym for *B*eing *A*ble *T*o *H*ear. I had so many things going on in my day that it was hard for me to wind down and sleep. Without sleep, I was restless and less effective during the next day, which produced a never-ending cycle of restlessness and added stress. By taking the time to start or end my day with a B.A.T.H., I'm able to hear, focus, and relax. In turn, it makes me more alert, more productive, and even more innovative.

Contents

Acknowledgments

One of the greatest lessons of my life is that if you want to go fast, go alone, but if you want to go far, go together. So goes the journey of writing a book. It is not a quick process, which is a good thing. Anything worth having is worth developing, especially if you plan to share it with the world. *S.K.I.R.T.S. in the Boardroom* is my first book, with many more to come. Publishing a book feels like watching a piece of fruit that takes forever to ripen. But the nourishment is necessary, and the pruning makes it more practical. Finally, its long-awaited time to be picked and showcased has arrived.

This is an accomplishment to be proud of, for sure, but it is certainly a community effort. I am blessed to have a wonderful community of champions. The sweetest victories are the ones that are shared. Were it not for the determination, generosity, patience, encouragement, commitment, and tireless efforts of the remarkable team and support system that assisted me with this project, the book would not be in your hands right now.

It is with deep gratitude that I express my appreciation to the following for their wonderful contributions:

◆ To my parents—my original team of make-it-happen supporters. To my mother, Mary Evans, for her encouragement, her prayers, her ear, and her advice. When you thought I wasn't listening and watching, I was paying attention! You've shown me what it means to mix style and substance and to be a woman that has it all. To my father, Carter Evans, for teaching me to dream big and for passing along the entrepreneurial, no-nonsense, getting-to-yes-is-the-only-option spirit! I'm fortunate to have you as a strong figurehead and as an example of how to dream bigger dreams. I'm incredibly proud of both of you and I deeply appreciate every sacrifice and every opportunity you gave me to succeed. Thank you.

◆ To my brother, Corey Evans. You are my best friend and my biggest supporter. I'm a better person because of your level-headedness and friendship. Despite being tackled and forced to run football routes, when I preferred to be at dance practice, I appreciate how you helped make me stronger—a strength that I try to share in this book. You came to pageants, twirling competitions, and recitals when I know you preferred to be shooting hoops or playing videogames. Your presence always has made—and always will make—a difference. Your best is yet to come.

- To my cousins Sean, Dimitri, Derek, Glen, Domenic, and Shomari, who founded B.A.M. (Boys Against Marshawn) and made me ready for battle at an early age! To the girls in my family, Ashley and Mollia, for being dynamic younger sisters. To my Great-Aunt Effie Jane for loving me like I was your daughter. And thank you to all of my aunts and uncles who have loved and supported me in more ways than words could express.

- To my longtime girlfriends—Tiffany Johnson, Karen Lyew, Nicky Black, Andrea Teague-Brown, Penny Muldrow, Kim Singleton, Erica Evans, and Cheri Miller. You are the most dynamic women I know and I appreciate your prayers and the example you set every day. And, to my little sister Treymayne Woodard.

- To my sisters from Texas Christian University—Nicole Williams, Lakayla Garrett, Consuela Holmes, Nicole Edwards, Lanasha Houze, and Yonina Robinson for being lifelong iron-sharpeners. And to my Georgetown University Law Center "Hoya Lawyer" sisters Cam Moultrie, Cloteen Bigger, Nicki Nelson, Tanya Goins, Carla Dorsey, Valerie Jackson, and Melanie Taylor.

- To one of my closest friends, Jason Illian. I'm so proud of all you've accomplished and I appreciate the years of prayers, encouragement, insight, and support. It's amazing to see how words spoken do not return void. I pray we both keep moving mountains.

- To my mentors: Gwen Wilson, at Verizon Wireless, thank you for making time for me; Mr. Larry Eger, my fifth-grade teacher, thanks for putting my name on the board less than any other teacher in my educational history and for teaching me to see myself through a lens of excellence; Janice Jackson, my twirling coach, who taught me about mental toughness in competition and in life; Yvonne Greenwood, my high school law magnet teacher, who opened doors for me to enter the legal profession with confidence at an early age; Dr. Donald Jackson, my TCU political science professor, who taught me to think outside the box and push the envelope; and Mr. Johnny Barnes, who unselfishly mentored me during my five years in Washington, D.C.

- To Raoul Davis, my manager, who first hinted that *S.K.I.R.T.S. in the Boardroom* was more than just a speaking topic, and to everyone at Ascendant Strategy Group/4th Dimension Management, including Annika Murray, Sherry Lloyd, Carlos Winston, and Davida Pitts. Thank you for believing in me. I look forward to what the future holds for us all.

- To my team at ME Unlimited and EDGE 3M Sports & Entertainment. Thank you to Renisha Jackson for all of your hard work and to Danielle Moss for going the extra mile. Special thanks to our designers, all of our vendors, and interns.

◆ To my editor Rusty Fisher—you're the best in the business. Anyone who "gets me," gets my utmost respect. To my literary agent, Bob Diforio, for your guidance and direction.

◆ Thank you to everyone at John Wiley & Sons, including Jessica Langan-Peck, Kim Dayman, Nick Snider, Amy Packard, and especially Shannon Vargo, for believing in the S.K.I.R.T.S. vision from the beginning.

◆ To my King of Hearts, Jason Robertson, who lifts me up with encouragement and provides me with a newfound balance as I seek to grow in my calling. Thank you for showing me how "it" should be.

◆ Most importantly, I thank the Lord of my life for the wonderful blessings He has bestowed, and for the opportunity to serve and advance the work of the Kingdom. I am Your workmanship created in You to do the good works You prepared in advance for me to do. I remain dressed and ready for service. I pray that Your light illuminates on every page.

Introduction
Not S.K.I.R.T.ing the Issue Anymore

Yes, that is me in the photo, posing with Donald Trump. And, yes, it is true that I was a contestant on the fourth season of *The Apprentice*. And, yes, I was lucky enough to have the opportunity to experience the ultimate business interview with Donald Trump himself on NBC's hit reality show.

And, yes, for 13 weeks, I went head-to-head with some of America's brightest, savviest business professionals. Did you know that I was the *only* woman during the season to lead The Donald's all-female team to a victory as the project manager for an upscale, yet in-your-face, advertising campaign for Lamborghini?

Figure I.1 The author with Donald Trump, who is no stranger to seeing S.K.I.R.T.S. in the boardroom.

The Apprentice was a great experience. I describe it as the ultimate crash-course MBA, and I loved it! You see, I actually crave (and thrive in) competitive, cut-throat, pressure-cooker situations! In order to be the best, you have to be willing to be challenged by the best. Given *my* reality as an entertainment attorney and the owner of both a performance strategy firm and a professional sports management and marketing company, I'm used to dealing with the big boys.

So why did I do the *Apprentice* in the first place, a show that had over one million applicants? In short, because I knew I could. It has expanded my purpose-driven platform to help empower, encourage, and equip women around the world to believe, boldly, in the power of their potential—and to *take no prisoners* in the process!

And, yes, I know what you're thinking, "Oh no; here it comes—another *Apprentice* contestant with another book about how great they are, what they learned from The Donald, yada, yada." But that's where you'd be wrong.

This is not a book about *The Apprentice*, or Donald Trump, or New York, or contestants. This is a book about success; success on your own terms in a world where being on a show like *The Apprentice* is not the summit of your achievements, but merely one more piece of the puzzle that makes you C.E.O. of *you*, of your career and your destiny. You see, a C.E.O. is my term for someone who Confidently Expects Opportunity—and knows how to capitalize on their talents, abilities, gifts, and skills to create a personal empire. America is a funny place; you can have a 4.0 grade point average, graduate summa cum laude from an Ivy League law school, win case after case, give back to your community, sit on boards and committees, and run multimillion-dollar companies—and all anyone wants to know about is your latest gimmick.

In my case, that would be *The Apprentice*. And don't get me wrong, I'm not complaining; if dropping The Donald's name helps me get a foot in the door without having to kick it down myself, I'm more than happy to do so. My cast made him tons of money in advertising and TV ratings anyway! The reason I don't mind is that I live a life of substance. There's plenty behind the door. I've been in boardrooms where more was on the line than getting fired by The Donald. I'm not being conceited. I'm just letting you know that I'm not a reality-TV-15-minutes-of-fame seeker.

In many ways, being a woman in today's business world is no different; you're held to a different, higher standard: In essence, what's your latest trick? You can't just do good, you have to look good; you can't just work hard, you've got to work twice as hard; you can't just show up, you have to show up early—and stay late.

It was no different when I was a runner-up for Miss America; people were much more interested in how I looked during the swimsuit competition than the content of the answers I gave during the interview portion of the program. I just so happened to win the interview *and* talent competition, and walked away with over $50,000 in scholarships to help pay my way through Georgetown University Law Center. But, hey, the swimsuit segment is more interesting! And I understand that. So it goes—and so it may always go. I could complain all day long, but the difference between a complaint and a suggestion is action—so I'd rather act to work within the system than whine about what's wrong with it.

So, if this book isn't about Donald Trump and *The Apprentice*, if it isn't about Miss America or swimsuits, if it's not about how much harder women have to work than men—and why that's just wrong—what *is* it about?

Well, actually, it *is* about all those things. It's about what I learned from 13 weeks on *The Apprentice*, what Donald *did* teach me, what being one of the top five Miss America finalists showed me about myself, and it's about how these competitions have affected my current, very successful business ventures in ways I could never have imagined.

More than anything, this is a book about vision: my vision, your vision, our vision.

See Your Future, Be Your Future

This book, *S.K.I.RT.S. in the Boardroom: A Woman's Survival Guide to Success in Business & Life*, is my vision for creating a more powerful, active, and realistic future for women just entering the mostly male-dominated corporate world. My perspective in *S.K.I.R.T.S.* is forward-thinking, and not entirely reflective. I'm under 30 years of age. So I'm not writing from the standpoint of managing a billion-dollar enterprise. My view is that of a young S.K.I.R.T. making a splash in significant ways.

Almost all women want to experience professional success. However, many find themselves unmotivated, unhappy, and unsatisfied. They are not alone. At the S.K.I.R.T.S. in the Boardroom: Set No Limits Seminar, you'll see that as women, we all want more, but wanting is not enough. At S.K.I.R.T.S. intensive seminars around the country, I always emphasize that to W.A.N.T. is really to experience *W*aiting, *a*nd *N*othing *T*ranspires. Usually, the problem is not desire. It's direction. Never before has there been a roadmap guiding women to navigate the perilous terrain of the corporate jungle—until now!

S.K.I.R.T.S. in the Boardroom is designed to equip women with the strategies necessary to combine confidence and compassion, style and substance, and, of course, beauty and brains. A must-have for all women looking to maximize their professional potential, *S.K.I.R.T.S. in the Boardroom* offers refreshing and inspiring business advice that is savvy, sensible, straightforward—and long overdue!

When Vision Becomes Reality

Many are called but few are chosen. The difference between the called and the chosen is that the chosen choose to answer. I've written *S.K.I.R.T.S. in the Boardroom* as an answer. In fact, I wrote it with you in mind. I know what it is like to fail, to be doubted and discouraged. But, I also know there is no problem that determination and direction cannot answer.

Being an ambitious, able, and assertive woman is no simple task—especially in what traditionally has been a man's world. However, you are the project manager, the director, the CEO, and the COO over every area of your life. Ultimately, you determine your success.

In essence, women asked me to write this book. For years, I have been traveling around the country speaking to corporations and college students. After many of my presentations, women (and some men!) asked if I planned on writing a book detailing the concepts and strategies discussed during my seminars or keynote speeches. I do not know everything there is to know about business. I'm not sure anybody really could.

However, I have gained wisdom from lessons learned over the years as an entrepreneur, a professional development and communication consultant, a corporate trainer, and as a lawyer. As an associate at a large corporate law firm, I learned about navigating a seemingly impossible web of politics to chart your own path. I learned a great deal about presence, poise, peak performance, and pressure as a former Miss District of Columbia and runner-up in the Miss America pageant. I learned about competition—and about working exclusively with women—during 13 weeks on *The Apprentice.*

And, in my current business venture as the president of EDGE 3M, a full-service media, marketing, and sports management firm (www.edge3m.com), I've learned that a woman's success is limited only by her unwillingness to adapt. In representing and elevating the brands of pro athletes in the NFL, NBA, and WNBA, I've landed some nice contracts, and lost some big ones as well. I've dealt with the challenges of being a woman in sports—and how that mirrors the challenges of being a woman in the boardroom.

I've secured some great endorsements for clients, and had deals that I thought were solid, but which completely fell through at the last minute. I've been underestimated and undermined. At the end of the day, it's all a part of business. I accept the bumps and bruises because I can honestly say I've had the chance to live many of my professional dreams. All of this taught me lessons to be shared in *S.K.I.R.T.S. in the Boardroom* and our S.K.I.R.T.S. in the Boardroom: Set No Limits Summit.

In my view, all women want to be successful. The opposite of success is failure. I refuse to believe that any woman hopes or wants to fail. Sometimes that happens—to all of us—but it is not a desire. If on one end of the spectrum we have success and on the other end failure, then that means there is a lot of room in between.

In the business world, this "room" feels like a corporate jungle. It is a jungle because, as women, we are in seemingly uncharted territory. It is only in recent years that women have begun to rightfully reign in the executive suite. Nonetheless, business is not easy. It can be ruthless, cutthroat, and unfair.

That said, it is a jungle for men, too. Many men, however, still see themselves as Tarzan—the fearless, adventurous hunter—and us as Jane. Quite frankly, I'm not exactly sure how to describe Jane's role. In the story, most of the emphasis is on Tarzan's brawn and Jane's beauty. I doubt Jane had a mentor! And that is the reason for this book.

The Boardroom

The boardroom is a place of power. It stands for any place, opportunity, or forum that is traditionally male-dominated. A place where big things happen, where decisions are made, deals are done and where you show what you're made of. The boardroom is your playing field, your court, your stage, your arena.

At different stages of life your boardroom will change. What it is today might be different from your boardroom of tomorrow. For me, it has been the classroom, the courtroom, the press room, and, now that I recruit pro athletes and their families, even the living room.

The boardroom is also a place where the good ol' boys network has, and continues to, flourish. It's our turn to take our seats in the executive suite. More specifically, it's YOUR turn. As women we face challenges every day. It's not about the challenges we face, however; it's about how we face them. So what's your boardroom?

S.K.I.R.T.S. in the Boardroom

I was raised around a lot of guys. I was the only girl. My brothers and cousins even started a club called BAM—*Boys Against Marshawn!* Most of my mentors have been males. This has made me an extreme alpha personality, and very competitive. Some women, and many men, view this competitive nature as a threat. It wouldn't be considered a threat in a man; it would be revered and praised. But as a woman, the alpha personality can often be seen as a liability. If I were to believe this, it would demean all that I've worked so hard to accomplish—and undermine all my future success.

Too many women are forced to navigate the perilous terrain of the corporate jungle with no guidance. For too long we have been forced to figure out how to survive on our own. The objective of *S.K.I.R.T.S. in the Boardroom* is to equip you with the tools necessary to chart your own course and fulfill your purpose. I will share with you the untold stories, secrets, and strategies that I, and some of America's top business professionals, have learned over the years. My hope is that this survival guide will help you to dream bigger dreams, and to dare.

Before we begin this journey together, I must share with you the meaning of the word S.K.I.R.T.S. It means more than just a garment. In the 1950s, the word *skirt* was often used to refer to a pretty girl—like the words *chick* or *dame*. *Skirt* can also mean "an edge" or "to miss." It's more complex than it first appears. The word has a history. It has evolved over the years, and has multiple meanings.

Wearing skirts, particularly in the business world, has been the subject of much debate—just like women. We are more than what we wear; and we are more than a word. We are more complex than we first appear. We have a rich history and have evolved with changing times. And our presence in the business world will always be the subject of much debate. In the context of this book, S.K.I.R.T.S. is actually an acronym that stands for women embracing the following qualities.

- ◆ **Sisterhood:** Women need to mentor and support one another's growth, while also learning to work together. Therefore, I don't mean sisterhood in the soft, fluffy sense. I mean it in the strong, focused sense. There is nothing wrong with soft and fluffy, but it's not a legitimate basis for professional success. Feminine is fine—nothing wrong with that, either. Heck, I still prep for a client meeting the same way I prepped for a Miss America interview. You can bet that my hair and makeup will be on point. I'm saying that there is tremendous value in helping other women learn the tricks of the trade as well. I'm not threatened by another woman's success—even a competitor's—instead, I see it as a challenge to improve myself. As the saying goes, if you want to go fast, go alone. If you want to go far, go together. That is what sisterhood, and this book, is all about.
- ◆ **Knowledge:** There is absolutely *no* substitute for knowledge; I don't believe anyone should "fake it 'til you make it" because, eventually, a lack of knowledge always comes back to haunt you. Besides, the more you know, the better you do. The better you do, the better you want to do. You dream bigger and *big* things happen. To be competitive, you must be aware of changes in the marketplace. What you don't know may not *directly* hurt you, but your competition surely will!
- ◆ **Integrity:** Ultimately, living a life of character, one defined by integrity and directed by values, is about living a life worthy of your calling. You

were created to build trust, show respect, set standards, and display honesty. What I call *next-level living*, or a lifestyle of success, becomes possible when we finally understand and embrace the fact that character is part of our calling.

◆ **Respect:** Respect is the gift that keeps on giving—the more you invest, the greater your ROI (return on investment). However, respect should be neither given nor taken too lightly. It is always a smart investment. As women we have a tendency to have misplaced trust *and* a lack of trust—particularly with other women. Developing a reputation as a person of integrity is invaluable. Respect is earned. Once you earn it and learn how to keep it, the world is your oyster. Lose it and you lose your ability to maximize your potential and capitalize on your greatest resource—relationships. In this book, I treat respect as the foundation on which success grows.

◆ **Tenacity:** To succeed at anything these days—in business, love, life, or the boardroom—you must absolutely be tenacious down to your very core. The world is moving so fast, in so many opposite directions, you have to absolutely hustle, persist, and stay abreast of ever-changing trends and information. Tenacity has six dimensions. It is the sum total of your desire, drive, determination, dedication, diligence, and discipline. The biggest fallacy is that the best comes to those who wait. Wrong! Those who wait play with the scraps leftover by those who hustle!

◆ **Substance:** What is substance? Substance is what's left when all the degrees, the pedigrees, the fashion, and the lipstick are stripped back to reveal the real you who is waiting—in some cases hiding—beneath. Whether your style is soft, subtle, and sweet or stern, sensible, and savvy, your substance is the essence of who you are. Many business authors, let alone CEOs, give substance short shrift; I make it a pivotal part of the *S.K.I.R.T.S. in the Boardroom* message, perhaps because it is the cornerstone of my own life.

I challenge you to keep each of the six core S.K.I.R.T.S. principles in mind as we develop together, chapter by chapter. This book as well as our S.K.I.R.T.S. in the Boardroom: Set No Limits Summit is about growth and guidance for dynamic women. Women just like you. It's fun, yet focused. I hope you will make a commitment to yourself to reflect upon the themes presented in each chapter by visiting www.skirtsintheboardroom.com at the end of each chapter's "Set No Limits" reflection. So, embrace your inner skirt, and let's get started!

Part One

From Chef to Chief Executive

The Difference Is a Little "I"

Part One focuses on four internal investments: the paradigms of confidence (self-esteem), class (attitude), course (direction), and commitment (dedication). Success begins within.

Chapter 1

Confidence

The Problem with Fake Eyelashes

Con•fi•dence (*n*) freedom from doubt; belief in yourself and your abilities.

Confidence. What a word. We hear it used often, tossed off like a pair of pantyhose with a run in it. It sounds good. We all know that it is important. But what does it really mean? This first chapter is the most extensive because it forms the foundation of everything else in the book. More importantly, confidence forms the foundation of everything in your life.

Hairpins

Confidence is like hairpins. Yes, hairpins. If you are from the South, like me, you might refer to these life-saving gems as bobby pins. Now, when you pick up a bobby pin, you can feel that it is pretty solid, although small. If you have ever used bobby pins, you know they pack a lot of potential! With just a little strategy and know-how, you can instantly obtain the look you want. But *only* if you position them in the right place.

I remember going to the hairdresser as a teenager to get ready for the prom. Of course, I wanted to look "mature," so I asked the stylist to put my hair in an "up-do." I have really thick hair! Whenever I tried to put up my own hair, I would use too many bobby pins and you could see them sticking out. However, my hairdresser knew exactly where to position each pin to give my hair the right amount of support.

It was not about how many pins she used—it was about how she used them. She used her teeth to change the shape of the pin depending on the type of reinforcement necessary. She had the uncanny ability to place them so that they were virtually invisible. And you know how important that is!

When I left the salon, my football-playing brother, Corey, asked how I managed to get my hair to stay up. The finished product really amazed him! He could see it, but he couldn't explain it. I responded with my pat answer for Corey: "None of your business!" First, he really did not care. Second, because it really *wasn't* his business!

When you have the perfect hairstyle, no one else needs to know how it got that way. In the same way that women have their own beauty secrets, it is also okay to have a silent sense of confidence. No one has the time or patience to hear about how many bobby pins you used, or how many times you tried before getting it right. Instead, they only see and care about the end result.

In our professional lives, obtaining and demonstrating confidence is very similar. Like a hairpin, it need not be very big or even noticeably visible to be effective. It is really not very important that others know how you got "it"—what is important is that you have it. Though it's not visible, *you* must know that it is there. That it provides you with the proper amount of support and reinforcement to give you the look— a.k.a., the self-assurance—that you desire. Without it you will be out of place—especially in the business world.

Confidence drives business. To be in the driver's seat, you must believe in your ability to make things happen. Otherwise, you are just along for the ride. You must also know that you have the ability to shape your confidence. My hairdresser used her teeth. You must use what you have. Use your gifts, your wisdom, and your talent.

> *Confidence is like hair. It grows stronger*
> *with proper conditioning.*
> —Marshawn Evans

A Cure for the Common Cold: *Insecurity*

Confidence is not optional—especially for women. We cannot succeed in a dog-eat-dog, cutthroat business world without it. The only way to climb the corporate ladder is to first have the confidence to take a step—then another step, and then another step.

The opposite of confidence, being secure, is insecurity. I know all about that. I have always been a fairly confident person—even as a kid. However, there were areas in which I was certainly less than confident. When I was in elementary school, I remember that every week a group of students would leave class to participate in a special program called REACH. Well, the REACH kids were known as the smart kids. At least, that's how I saw them.

They had taken a special aptitude test, one that I don't remember taking, which enabled them to go to this mysterious place—a place that I knew absolutely nothing about. (At the time I called it "Never, Never Land" because I *never* got to go there!) All I knew was that I was not a part of the school's designated "smart-kid" clique. Being excluded had a tremendous impact on my academic self-esteem. From that point onward, I did not see myself as smart—at least not as smart as the other kids. I did fine in school, but not great. I never challenged myself, and I did just enough to get by.

As I entered junior high and high school, my leadership qualities began to flourish, and I started my first real business as the host of several dance and modeling camps. I was a freshman cheerleader, the high school band's featured baton twirler, first runner-up in the Miss Teen Texas pageant, and an officer in over a dozen student groups. I was making straight A's, but year after year, my teachers would encourage me to take honors and advanced placement courses. I was sure they were mistaken.

I understand how they might be confused. After all, I was making really high grades, but they did not understand. My thinking was that I made good grades because I worked hard, not because I was smart. No matter how hard I worked, certain areas were still out of my reach. When asked to take the advanced courses, I reverted back to being the elementary school girl left at her desk while the smart kids went off to Never, Never Land.

Thankfully, my high school teachers' persistence paid off. In my senior year, I made myself take all honors and advanced placement classes. What a way to spend senior year! However, I learned that stretching your confidence is not about how you feel. It's about how you focus. Stepping outside of your comfort zone will rarely *feel* good. It actually feels unnatural, which can be intimidating. That is when you defer to your head, and not your heart.

The "stretch" of the academic challenges changed my shape for the better. I ended up graduating with honors in the top 5 percent of my high school class and was accepted by almost every school to which I applied.

I wish I could say that was the end of the story. That fall I went off to college. During the middle of my first semester, I received a letter in the mail. It was a beautiful invitation on fancy paper from the Honor's Department at Texas Christian University. I read it, but had no intentions of responding. Again, they must have been mistaken, too.

High school honor courses were one thing, but college was a completely different story. Or so I thought. For some reason, I mentioned the letter to my father. Between the two of us, he was easily more enthusiastic. I was content with getting the invitation. I tried to explain to him why I was not fit for the program. In my view, I was not the type of person for this program. Only the really "smart" ones could keep up and do well in a collegiate honors curriculum. I mean, hey, the reality is that some people can shop at S, and others can only afford Sack 'n' Save. There's nothing wrong with either store. I just wasn't the type, and that's all there was to it. (Sigh!) While my father heard me, he would not listen.

Dad tried to encourage me, but nothing he said would change my mind. So, he upped the ante! He agreed to pay the expenses for me to have my own dorm room for the next semester. (I had a messy roommate—bless her heart—sweet, but messy.) And, that's all she wrote!

I enrolled in the honors program. The honors classes were challenging, but I was able to pull A's in those classes, too. I finished *magna cum laude* with honors and distinction. I became a Truman Scholar, one of *Glamour* magazine's Top Ten College Women, and a *USA Today* Academic First Team member. Plus, I received nearly $200,000 in academic scholarships. Ha! Yes, me—the same girl who was not in the REACH classes.

I learned that another person's opinion about you is never as important as your opinion about you. I also learned that I could rise to any challenge *if* I had the right frame of mind. Beauty industry pioneer Mary Kay Ash once taught that whether you think you can or can't, you are right either way. Confidence is not just about how you feel about yourself. It is also about your focus—how you think. It's amazing what you can see when you choose what *not* to look at. As the saying goes, some can't see the forest for the trees.

Today, it is hard to believe that I once had a case of academic insecurity. Insecurity is a common ailment that many women deal with. It is a condition that can go undiagnosed for far too long if you are not careful. On my journey to the Miss America competition, I was constantly under the microscope. There was no shortage of people who were eager to be the movie critic for my personal life story. I was too tall, too thin, eyes too big, hair too thick, or my suit was the wrong color. The list goes on and on.

I learned that opinions are just that—opinions are based on one person's point of view. Nothing more, nothing less. Opinions are not facts. Just as people can be right, they can also be wrong. One of the keys to professional success is learning to place the opinions, doubts, and comments expressed by others in perspective.

During my first semester at Georgetown University Law Center, I considered enrolling in Georgetown's joint degree program. I wanted to obtain my law degree and my MBA at the same time. So, I went to an information meeting about the school's joint degree offerings. Before law school, I had a pretty extensive background in politics and youth development. I had been the national spokesperson for the Invest in Youth Campaign, named by the Texas governor to the state's Juvenile Justice Advisory Board, and co-founder of the National Youth Network under the U.S. Justice Department. I went to law school, in part, to diversify my experiences. I always wanted to be an attorney, but I still had a passion and a knack for business.

After the presentation, I was even more interested in the JD-MBA. I approached the law center's dean of admissions and told him about my interests. I was expecting him to match my enthusiasm with words of encouragement. Instead, he paused for a moment, wrinkled his face like he had just eaten a piece of bad fruit, titled his head, and said something that still sticks with me to this day: "Well, you might want to think about that. I mean, the business school is for people who have been in the business world operating at pretty high levels for quite some time. I'm not saying you *shouldn't* do it, but the principles—especially the accounting—are extremely complex. These guys are some heavy hitters." He went on to say that maybe I should enroll in the joint MPA—Masters in Public Administration. *Humph.*

Like that, with only a few short (and really discouraging!) words, this man caused me to doubt my ability. It was very clear from his body language and his statements that he didn't think I was suited for a Georgetown MBA. Now, I don't know whether he had any bad intentions or realized the impact of his words, but, because he was a part of the recruitment team, I valued his opinion. My mistake was in placing *too* much value in—overvaluing—his opinion. Looking back at it now, I now see that it was a dumb opinion. You see, before law school, I had already operated my own consulting company and had done more before the age of 21 than many in business school had done by the age of 30.

I don't regret not enrolling in business school. I *do* regret listening to one man's dumb opinion. (I'll explain why I keep calling his opinion dumb.) I've now learned to place the opinions of others in perspective. No matter what phase you're experiencing in your life, and no matter how much you've accomplished (I was already a Georgetown law student, for heaven's sake!), people will still tell you that you cannot or should not attempt something—that you are striving or reaching too high. (Is that even possible?) Remember, no one knows your potential the way you do. They don't know your visions, your passion, and your purpose. So they are making uninformed—a.k.a. "dumb"—statements.

The reality is that women are rarely encouraged to go into business. We have to make that choice for ourselves. Thankfully, I had enough drive to press onward and achieve some pretty neat things in spite of Dean Dumbo (I've changed the dean's name to protect his identity; it's just between us girls, anyway). In my world, I deal with professional athletes and sports agents. As an attorney, I represented Fortune 500 companies at my law firm. I deal with heavy hitters and the big boys every day.

There is an important lesson here: Another person's opinion of you cannot define you without your permission. Regardless of the type of insecurity you may be dealing with, or not dealing with, there is a cure. Confidence. In order for it to work, you have to be willing to write your own prescription.

> *It took me a long time not to judge myself*
> *through someone else's eyes.*
> —Sally Field

Behind the Mascara

Empty confidence is like a pair of cheap pantyhose. You buy them expecting to wear them one or two times. If they snag right away, you are not surprised. The quality was poor in the first place. What is worse is if you are at a business meeting and you get a run. You know, a snag that starts small but by the end of the day grows as big as a convention hall. You cannot concentrate because all you can think about is your run.

If you are resourceful, you can use hairspray or clear nail polish to stop the run. Hopefully it will buy you some time, but not much. You have to watch every step you take and all your movements to make sure the run does not get any worse. After all, you do not want the whole world to see that unsightly tear.

The same is true for empty confidence. When we lack confidence, we become obsessed with what others think. We don't want others to see the "run" in our self-esteem, so we cover it up and try to distract people in hopes that they will not notice. More plainly, as women we tend to hide behind designer suits, false eyelashes, advanced degrees, a big check, and a nice car.

All can become disguises for true confidence—concealers that hide our imperfections. These things may bolster your self-esteem for a while, but they will never give you fulfillment or sustained self-assurance. You may even try to distract others with the way you talk or by being boastful. Confidence is not always spoken. The real deal is usually silent.

Most successful women have a magnetic quality about them. You do not *see* their confidence, you *sense* it. You cannot put your finger on it, but you know it is there. Think about a woman whom you admire, someone who epitomizes strength and assurance.

If I were a betting woman, I would bet that she never boasts about her accomplishments. There is a reason for that. She knows who she is and that's that. Others naturally see and are drawn to her confidence. Why? Confidence is a magnet. Insecurity, on the other hand, demagnetizes attraction. What energy are you giving?

From the Inside Out

To be the cream that rises to the top of the corporate ladder, you have to standout. One of the things that we emphasize at the S.K.I.R.T.S. in the Boardroom: Set No Limits Summit is that there is too much competition for you to expect to excel if you always blend in. There has to be something different about you that enables you to get different opportunities. That something begins with confidence. Your confidence will attract new opportunities.

Did You Know?
More women than men earn master's degrees.
                    (*Source:* Voice of America radio broadcast)

Confidence and conceit are not one and the same. A conceited person is arrogant, which is offensive. It demagnetizes right away because conceit is a sign of low self-esteem. Conceited people have something to prove—or at least they think they do. They are actually trying to hide insecurity.

Remember, you have nothing to prove to anyone. When you lack confidence, you waste your time trying to get others to think you are secure, that you have it all together—that there is no RUN (Real-life Unpredictable Nonsense) in your pantyhose—I mean, in your life. The truth is you do not have it all together. Honey, no one does! And I am here to tell you it is perfectly okay.

We have all been there. *No one—not even a man—has it all together.* Everyone has problems. Everyone has insecurities. Everyone has made mistakes, including you and me. We don't have to announce it on the front page of the *New York Times* or air it on the daytime talk show *The View*, but we do have to be real with ourselves. We can keep it between us girls. That's not a problem. My point is that building confidence requires you to be honest with yourself about your insecurities and strengths.

Going back to my Georgetown experience, I began to realize that there was a pattern. At every major stage of life, something or someone popped up and tried to discourage me from moving to the next level. Each time I had a choice. Play it safe, or step out on faith. It's like coming to a fork in the road. You decide which way you will go. Allowing someone else's opinion to guide you is like letting someone else decide your direction, your path, and your journey. It's not their call. It's yours.

The bigger lesson is that these obstacles or fork-in-the-road moments *never* go away. Just as they've appeared at every major phase of my life in the past, those same roadblocks will continue to appear in the future. As I'll say several times, it's not the challenges you face, it's how you face them. You *can* approach these fork-in-the-road moments with boldness. Why? Because that is what you were designed to do. That is what next-level living is all about.

The reality is that we have all been down the wrong path. We've listened to wrong people, missed out on great opportunities, or played it just a little too safe. You know what? That doesn't make you a failure; it just makes you human.

The good news is that nothing can ever decrease your value. No matter what you've been through—if you been fired, downsized, demoted, divorced, or dumped—your value is the same. You were still created on purpose, with purpose, for a purpose. You are here for a reason. As humans, we can go through adversity and changes without losing our value.

Your car loses its value the moment you drive it off the lot. Its value decreases dramatically if you are in an accident. A stock portfolio can take a hit, and, even if it rises, the confidence of others in the stocks may never be the same.

So many things lose commercial value. (Can you say burst real-estate bubble?) But not you. Your value never decreases. In fact, it cannot decrease because you were already created with infinite value, worth, and possibility. You are worth the promotion. You are worth the new contract. You are worth more than you can imagine.

We Need You

I'll say it one more time: You are here for a reason. You are in the boardroom, at the table, in your office, or in your executive position for a reason. The specific reason will vary—you will have to listen to yourself. But, the ultimate reason is universal. You are here because your presence is necessary.

Think about that: *You are needed.* You are the answer to someone's question, and the solution to someone's problem. Your value is of immeasurable worth. You add to this world. You add to your corporate environment. Your presence simply adds—you are needed.

Insecurity only takes away from your effectiveness—your ability to perform and to add value. This happens when we doubt ourselves. The result is that we actually detract from ourselves and, in turn, from others.

Having confidence is absolutely necessary. It is fundamental that you understand who you are and embrace who you are. There is no one else with your DNA. No one else with your fingerprints. That means no one is carrying the same goods that you've got. And, sister, no one else in this universe can leave a mark the way that you can.

> *And as we let our own light shine, we unconsciously give*
> *other people permission to do the same. As we are liberated*
> *from our fear, our presence automatically liberates others.*
> —Marianne Williamson

The Four Spheres of Confidence

I mentioned that confidence is a word that is tossed about, much like a cliché. This book is not about show. It is about substance. So, now that

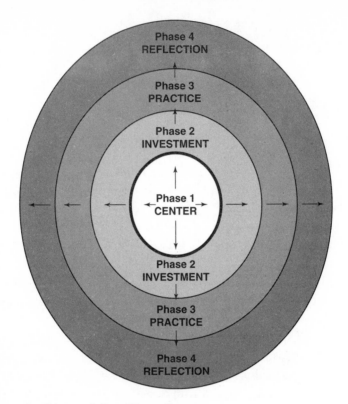

Figure 1.1 Confidence: A Four-Phrase Process

I've set the stage by discussing the importance of having confidence, let me share with you how to get it and grow it.

Confidence is the by-product of four phases: phase one is CENTER; phase two is INVESTMENT; phase three is PRACTICE; and phase four is REFLECTION. See Figure 1.1, which demonstrates this concept visually.

True confidence is built and destroyed internally—by you! Not by others. Confidence is a series of investments. You can also look at confidence as a series of choices you choose to make about life. What you choose to believe about yourself impacts your confidence. In the chart, you will see that each sphere of confidence grows based upon choices that you make.

You have to have confidence in your ability, and then be tough enough to follow through.
—Rosalynn Carter

Confidence Phase One: *Center*

At the core, your sense of confidence begins *in* you. What you *believe* about yourself matters. What you *say* about yourself matters. And how you *see* yourself matters. The way in which you characterize each of these three issues determines the core foundation of your confidence— what you believe, say, and see about yourself. A solid core leads naturally to solid growth.

Think about an apple. Before it becomes fruit, it begins as a seed. That seed first produces and strengthens the core of the apple before it expands. Our confidence grows in the same way. It grows outward from the center. As long as the core is healthy, the remaining layers have a foundation upon which to build, expand, and bear fruit.

A seed is also full of potential. What it looks like now is no indication of what it will be in the future. You might see a seed. I see a forest. That is how expansive your potential is, too. At the core of who you are lie several seeds of potential waiting to blossom.

We either cap, or uncap, our potential based on the expectations we set for ourselves. Your actions will inevitably reflect your expectations. Similarly, your actions are limited or expanded based on your expectations. If you always see yourself as an assistant and you expect to remain an assistant, it is almost certain that you will always be an assistant. Now, there is nothing wrong with that. It is, however, a choice based on the expectations you set for yourself.

Your expectations are a direct reflection of your confidence—the degree to which you have embraced your potential. It is imperative that you believe you are wonderfully made, and that you were born with greatness inside. You automatically expect to strive for the best. However, if you do not have that fundamental picture of yourself, it is as though you were ignoring your potential and allowing it to lie dormant. Everything else you do in life will be limited by low self-esteem and low expectations.

A Word about Excellence and Football

What words or synonyms come to mind when you think of excellence? When I think of the word excellence, I think of something or someone reflecting the finest in quality. Think about the greatest speech or the best performance you have ever experienced—something that truly moved, mesmerized, or motivated you. You might characterize that experience by saying something like, "Wow! That was *excellent*!" Or, you may say something else. Let's see exactly what you would you say.

Take a moment, close your eyes and *really* think about that experience. I want you to describe the experience by filling in the blank and substituting a word of your choice for the word "excellent."I will give you three tries (three is my favorite number!), so be creative.

Example 1: "Wow! That was _____."

Example 2: "Wow! That was _____."

Example 3: "Wow! That was _____."

Keep in mind there are no right or wrong answers. When I filled in the blanks, I thought of three words: "exceptional," "invaluable," and "quality." Now, I want you to take your three words, and insert them into these sentences.

"I am _____."

"I am _____."

"I am _____."

"I am exceptional. I am invaluable. I am quality." I *love* how that sounds. You see, I will admit that this is how I see myself. While I do not hold myself as the gold standard for success and excellence, I am not ashamed to say that I am an achiever . . . a winner . . . and a dominator. I was born to be excellent. And, I won't apologize for being great!

If I were anything less, then I would owe you an apology for not living up to my value. I am exceptional. I am invaluable. I am quality. And, I don't merely say these things. That's what I believe, and that's how

I live. My perception of myself influences how others see me at work and in the boardroom. It shapes my confidence, and it shows.

Most extraordinarily successful women already see themselves as excellent—not necessarily perfect, but great nonetheless. Defining excellence as a way of life begins with determining how you see yourself. Your picture of yourself determines your performance throughout the game of life.

Did You Know?
Secretary of State and former National Security Adviser Condoleezza Rice lists her dream job as being commissioner of the NFL.

I think sports are a metaphor for life. Plus, as the owner of a marketing and sports management agency, sports pays my bills! So I will use football to illustrate how your self-image impacts your performance.

Chance is a quarterback for a Division 1 college football team. His teammates and coaches recognize his talent, quickness, and athleticism. However, they do not trust him in pressure situations, or when the game is on the line. Chance has a focusing problem. He constantly compares himself to his competition, and tends to focus on the abilities of others rather than his own. *He* thinks he is slow. *He* thinks his talent is just average. *He* thinks he is never quite ready. A new season is here, but Chance cannot get past last season.

During the last season, Chance's team had an opportunity to win the national championship. His team was fourth and inches. In football-friendly terms, that means they were *really* close to scoring and winning the whole game.

The center (the really big guy who allows the quarterback to put his hands—well, you know where) snapped the ball, but no receiver was open. Chance, the quarterback, decided to scramble and run the ball in for a touchdown. Out of nowhere, BOOM! He got the daylights knocked out of him, and he fumbled the ball. His team lost. Chance lost a lot more than just the game with that hit. To this day, he still sees himself as a fumbler. His perception or picture of himself continues to influence his performance.

The moral of the story is that Chance allows defeat to define him. This story *could* have gone another way. Chance could have looked back at the circumstances and said to himself, "Well, at least I'm a fighter—if I'm going down, I'm doing so with a bang!" Dare I imagine what Chance's performance would look like now if he saw himself as a fighter as opposed to a fumbler? It is a matter of perspective and self-perception.

In business, your *perception* of yourself matters. It matters if you see yourself as tenacious versus timid, or assertive versus apprehensive. Image *is* everything. It is true. After all, image begins with the letter "I."

Self-*perception* matters. What you *say* about yourself matters. Most importantly, what you *believe* about yourself matters. Do you see yourself as excellent? As exceptional, invaluable, quality, or any of the three words you chose to insert? Do your words and thoughts reflect the resilient buoyancy and faith of a fighter, or the regretful fear of a fumbler?

Confidence Phase Two: *Investment*

Confidence is the result of a series of internal investments. The most important investment a person can make is in themselves. In order to succeed, you need others to invest in you, too. Most failures occur because of a lack of planning and preparedness. If you fail to plan, then you plan to fail.

Self-image and self-perception, how you see yourself, determines your confidence, which, in turn, determines your actions. And it determines the type of investments you are willing to make in your life. Our self-image is a direct reflection of our confidence.

Confidence increases as we increase our capacity to excel. We do this by making investments in self. When you go to school, you expand your capacity with additional knowledge. When you attend a corporate training or a seminar, you expand your capacity. When you develop stronger communication skills, you expand your capacity.

When you learn how to interact efficiently with your co-workers, you expand your capacity. When you develop a stronger sense of character, guess what? You expand your capacity. I could go on and on. We have the opportunity to expand (or retract) our capacity based on the investments in ourselves we choose to make, or choose not to make.

When you make investments in yourself, you instantaneously expand your capacity to excel.

Capacity is another word for *potential*—your ability to maximize your gifts. When you have great potential that grows greater because of quality investments that are made, you increase your confidence. A woman who looks at herself and is not only aware of her potential, but *consciously* and *consistently* develops, nurtures, and embraces that potential is fierce! She epitomizes confidence.

> *I think the key is for women not to set any limits.*
> —Martina Navratilova

Know Who You Are

Who you are is based on what's inside. A container is only as valuable as its contents. What is in your container? What are you investing? Our deposits make us confident of our ability to make a withdrawal.

When we go to the bank, we make a deposit. We put money in our account so that when we need to make a withdrawal we have sufficient funds. However, many times as women we do not make the proper investments in ourselves. Therefore, when it comes time for a promotion or a new opportunity, we have NSF—nonsufficient funds. We are not ready. We want promotion without preparation. You have to crawl before you can walk. You have to walk before you can strut—especially in stilettos.

As women, we sometimes fail to make the proper deposits. There are a few reasons for this. First, we may tend to see ourselves as bank tellers, not depositors. What in the world am I talking about?! Let me explain. The role of a bank teller is to facilitate monetary transactions. A bank teller can only do what he or she is told.

For instance, when you go to deposit your check you instruct the bank teller as to how much you want deposited. You specify the accounts, and what you say goes. They, by nature of their job, can only follow instructions, not give them.

If you ask a teller to do something they are not authorized to do, that person must go to his or her boss for direction on how to handle the situation. A teller is surrounded by thousands, if not millions, of dollars every single day. But he or she has no control over where it goes. As women, we often see ourselves as tellers—as facilitators or intermediaries. We are content with following directions, not giving them.

My point is that we are often content with being near the action, not controlling it. Contentment extinguishes the need for continued action. You are happy where you are. You are happy being directed; therefore, you do not make investments in yourself to increase your net worth.

Stated more plainly, if you lack confidence and doubt your ability to get a promotion, to become a CEO, or to master the tasks before you, you stop trying. If you do not believe in your ability to obtain a desired end, you will rarely prepare properly. You will become content based on insecurity. Now, if you are content, make sure it is for the right reasons. If it is based on fear, you are selling yourself short.

Your confidence in your ability to reach the finish-line influences *how* you decide to run the race. When you see yourself as a depositor rather than a teller, your perspective is wholly different. You write the check; you decide the amount. You authorize the bank to make the payments. You are in control. Similarly, you are in control of *you*. You decide if and how you will grow professionally.

If you expect high returns, you make solid investments. You are not content with simply being a part of the transaction; you make steps to benefit from it. You are a depositor. Treat the development of your confidence like the development of your career—as a wise investment.

Confidence Phase Three: *Practice*

After researching, observing, and learning from "great" people over the years, I have discovered that "greatness" develops one choice at a time. It is not an overnight phenomenon. As for those who achieve overnight success, they often lose it shortly thereafter. It is true that anything worth having is worth working for. It is the process that produces a powerful skills set—skills that will sustain success. The process also serves to refine our sense of confidence.

I look at personal and professional development the same way that I look at diamonds. When found in nature, diamonds are rough and uneven. To maximize and reveal their true value, the diamond must be cut and polished.

All of us start as diamonds in the rough—unrefined, uncut, unpolished, but full of valuable potential. We, too, have to be sanded and polished to reveal our true potential. Although it is a necessary part of life, that does not mean we like the way development feels. It means you will have to go through some challenging experiences; but that is the only way to win.

The refinement phases of practice and preparation give us confidence to excel. We prepare by becoming good at what we do. It enables us to step onto the playing field. Practice may not make perfect, but it increases our odds of coming close.

I travel the country giving seminars and speeches. A few years ago, I founded a company called Communication Counts! and conducted presentations on public speaking, interviewing, and communication. Why? Simple: Many people are terrified at the idea of speaking in public.

Believe it or not, some rank it above the fear of dying! I enjoy sharing thoughts and ideas with audiences; however, I was not always comfortable speaking in public. I used to walk up to the podium with my microphone shaking in one hand, and my written speech shaking in the other. It was not about my *ability* to be a good speaker. It was about my perception of myself. I labeled myself as a novice and that was reflected in my performance.

There were two other reasons for my nervousness. First, I had never been in a position to deliver speeches before, so I did not know what I was doing. Second, I hated to practice. With little or no practice, I was not prepared. When it came time to perform, the lack of preparation showed. Practice and preparation always enhances your self-perception. Your picture of yourself is tied directly to your performance.

Now, I prepare for my speeches in advance. I also get lots of practice by being on the road. That practice combined with proper preparation for each engagement produces a strong sense of confidence. Feel free to book my company for a speaking engagement if you want to see for yourself!

More Practice

The first time I stepped into a courtroom as a lawyer, I was in new territory. I was somewhat anxious, but I knew how to handle it. I researched the law and investigated the case. I formulated my questions and drafted my opening and closing statements.

I did my best to anticipate any potential curveballs that the other side or the judge might throw. And, I practiced, practiced, practiced. I performed a series of mental rehearsals by seeing myself in the courtroom and visualizing a successful delivery with confidence and authority. I also practiced out loud.

I practiced entering evidence and making objections. To me this was like preparing for a speech, only this time it would be more interactive— and there was a lot more on the line. The formula for success was the same: practice and preparation. It always boosts your confidence. And I won the case!

Let me digress for a moment to point out that I never gave much attention to mistakes. I did not see myself stumbling. Focusing on that would only increase my likelihood of stumbling. I learned this lesson the hard way, while at the Miss America competition. For the talent portion, I performed a rhythmic dance twirl for my talent. It was a baton-twirling routine.

Being a twirler was one of the most mentally challenging skills of my life. If I messed up by dropping the baton, there was no hiding it— everyone would know it. And no one would let me live it down. Trust me! I became very good over the years, competing at international events. I would have excellent practices, but when it was time to perform, when it really mattered, my mind could not focus properly. I kept thinking about how I did not want to make mistakes. By doing so, oddly enough, my mind was actually focusing on mistakes. That thought process impacted my performance.

That is, until I learned the power of mental rehearsal. By focusing on positive outcomes, you increase the likelihood of positive outcomes. You build your confidence with thoughts of succeeding. Think about it. Have you ever walked down the street in a new pair of heels and thought about not tripping? What happened? Naturally, you tripped!

Our actions, consciously or subconsciously, follow our thoughts. We spend a lot of time dealing with confidence during our S.K.I.R.T.S. in the Boardroom: Set No Limits Summit, where you can learn about experimental techniques to apply these principles, which will increase your confidence. We help you rewire your subconscious to trust your instincts. Finally, for those of you who may have smiled or chuckled at my Miss America talent (baton-twirling), that is okay! I will have you know that I won the talent competition at Miss America, and ended up with over $50,000 in scholarship money. I was smiling, too, but for a different reason!

Business Boosters

I have found over the years that practice (mental rehearsal and actual repetition) combined with preparation boosts your confidence in business as well. I go to gazillions of conferences every year. I always research who is going to be at the conference, and I even practice what I might say.

Practicing my pitch to potential clients in advance helps me come across with confidence and authority. Being able to sell my idea is just as important as being able to sell myself. People do business with people they like and trust. I do not sound rehearsed, but I do sound as if I know what I am talking about.

Many people are very talented, but lose deals because they fail to properly prepare. When you practice, you not only build internal confidence, but the practice manifests externally as well, so that others have confidence in you, too.

Successful business developers—or *rainmakers*, as we call them in the legal profession—are those who can generate new clients and opportunities. Every deal is a new deal, and every client is a new client. Preparing yourself by practicing your approach and becoming good at what do boosts your confidence, which boosts business.

The biggest room is the room for improvement.
—Mary Evans (Mom)

Confidence Phase Four: *Reflection*

The key to continued growth is learning from your experiences. Once you know who you are (step one), consistently make investments in yourself (step two), and practice to perfect your technique and skill (step three), then you have to take the time to reflect upon what you have learned (step four). Knowledge is power, right? When you take the time to learn about yourself, you equip for yourself for the next test.

As a first-year law student, I was fortunate to receive two offers from large law firms to work as a summer associate. Most law firms only hire second-year law students, so I was on cloud nine with two offers in my pocket. What most people do not realize is that I got over 100 rejection letters! That's a lot of rejection! Interestingly, all of those rejections opened the door for a lot of reflection.

With every "no," I learned what it took to get a "yes." Most people would have given up after the first 50 rejections. Giving up was not an option. I wanted the experience and the paycheck. I made a lot of money that summer. I made even more the following summer.

The next year, I had 20 offers from firms all over the country, all paying six figures. I reflected upon every rejection; I learned from my mistakes. I learned what the recruiters were looking for, and what information to include in a cover letter and during an interview.

In most instances, the timing was not right the first time around. By round two, I was way ahead of my competition and my colleagues because I had been through the process before. Most of my fellow law students had not.

Reflection builds confidence. Sometimes mistakes and rejection can be the best thing that can ever happen to you, if your perspective is properly aligned. When you make a mistake, make sure to learn from it. If you learn from your mistakes, you will know what not to do. In business, that is half of the battle.

A woman is like a tea bag. You never know how strong she is
until she gets into hot water.
—Eleanor Roosevelt

Confidence is more than a word. It is a way of life. When confidence truly becomes a way of life, it determines your lifestyle. However, when it is simply a word, it is disposable, replaceable, and shakable.

In order to survive in the business world, a confident style *must* be a part of your lifestyle. It will not reflect around you until it first begins inside you. So, get your bobby pins ready. . . only the ones you need. And, throw those torn pantyhose out for good. No more quick fixes with hairspray or clear nail polish. Let's start with a brand new designer pack.

Lessons for ME (Motivation & Empowerment)

A confident style is a lifestyle developed in four phases:

1. *Phase one is your CENTER:* Your confidence is SOLID because you have a strong self-image. You know who you are, what you are made of, and what you have to offer. Others' opinions about you do not influence your perception of yourself.

2. *Phase two is based on your INVESTMENT:* Your confidence is SECURE because you build it upon a firm foundation of sound investments and internal deposits. Every investment is another brick laid.

3. *Phase three comes from PRACTICE:* Your confidence is SEA-SONED because you have gained the experience necessary to develop expertise. You have become good at what you do. With knowledge comes boldness.

4. *Phase four springs from REFLECTION:* Your confidence is SAVVY. Now you have the know-how and the knowledge, to play the game. You learn from all of your experiences, good and bad.

Set No Limits Reflection

I think it's important to reflect on any lesson before moving on, and particularly on the subject of this first chapter—confidence).That is why I've designed this last section of each chapter as a specific time for both reflection and action, as you are asked to not only answer each question but also to actively write your answer down. You can explore more reflective insights on this topic at www.skirtsintheboardroom.com. I hope you find the process as beneficial as I do.

PHASE ONE: CENTER
What five words describe you, and why?

    5. _____

    6. _____

    7. _____

    8. _____

    9. _____

What makes you unique?

    1. _____

    2. _____

    3. _____

What are your best personal qualities?

    1. _____

    2. _____

    3. _____

What are your best qualities professionally?

    1. _____

    2. _____

    3. _____

Why do you deserve to be successful in business?

1. _____

2. _____

3. _____

What situations make you insecure? What causes the insecurity?

Insecure Situations	*Insecurity Causes*
1. _____	*1.* _____
2. _____	*2.* _____
3. _____	*3.* _____
4. _____	*4.* _____
5. _____	*5.* _____

What situations make you confident? What contributes to your confidence?

Confident Situations	*Confident Causes*
1. _____	*1.* _____
2. _____	*2.* _____
3. _____	*3.* _____
4. _____	*4.* _____
5. _____	*5.* _____

PHASE TWO: INVESTMENT

What investments have you already made in yourself? What benefits do you hope to gain?

1. _____
2. _____
3. _____
4. _____
5. _____

What investments do you need to make *personally*? When will you begin?

Personal Investments	*Timeline*
1. _____	1. _____
2. _____	2. _____
3. _____	3. _____
4. _____	4. _____
5. _____	5. _____
6. _____	6. _____
7. _____	7. _____

What investments do you need to make *professionally*? When will you begin?

Professional Investments	*Timeline*
1._____	1._____
2._____	2._____
3._____	3._____
4._____	4._____
5._____	5._____
6._____	6._____
7._____	7._____

PHASE THREE: *PRACTICE*

What areas in my professional life can become stronger with more practice and better preparation?

1. _____

2. _____

3. _____

4. _____

5. _____

6. _____

7. _____

8. _____

9. _____

10. _____

PHASE FOUR: *REFLECTION*

What lessons can I learn from my past experiences and mistakes? How can I use these lessons to my advantage?

1. _____

2. _____

3. _____

4. _____

5. _____

6. _____

7. _____

8. _____

9. _____

10. _____

Chapter 2

Class

Attitude, Mixed with a Pinch of Allure,
Determines Your Altitude

Class (*adjective*) highly stylish; elegant.

What is the first thing you notice about a woman? Is it her hair? Her shoes? Her purse? Nope. Maybe her confidence? Close. It's her attitude. Attitude is the first thing others will notice, and the last thing others will remember.

In fact, your attitude (whether you realize it or not) is your trademark. At ME Unlimited, our agency focuses on performance strategy. We emphasize, heavily, the importance of "attitude" as an essential value-add, and a necessary part of professional, yet feminine, allure and assertiveness. Long gone are the days of being a bubbly blonde or beautiful brunette as the key to standing out. Getting noticed (and being taken seriously) is about what substance and perspective you have to offer, *and* what bottom-line value you can add to your company or your customers.

Your Most Valuable Accessory

Clearly, attitude is important. I would even go so far as to say that it is *everything*. Attitude sets the tone for all of your relationships and interactions. The empowering thing about attitude is that it is completely within our control. No one else determines what I think, feel, say, or do.

29

Other factors might influence me, but I'm in control of my attitude. And, whether you fully realize it or not, you're in control of your attitude as well.

Understand that attitude is a choice. Just like you choose which skirt you are going to wear with your red power-pumps, you choose which attitude you are going to wear with your daily circumstances.

As women, we spend lots of time looking in the mirror and making sure that everything about our appearance looks just right. I know I do. We should spend the same amount of time, if not more, making sure that the most important aspect of the impression, influence, and ultimate impact we make on the world around us is just right, too.

Know Your M.O.

The term *M.O.* is short for the Latin term *modus operandi*. This essentially refers to a person's habitual or standard mode or method of operation. We all have an M.O. that is reflected every day by our attitude. Attitude is a reflection of how you operate and how you react. It influences whether or not people want to work with you, want to do business with you, want to promote you, or even hire you in the first place. It tells the world who you are and how you approach life—especially adversity.

Like a signature scent, your attitude either emits an appealing fragrance, or, well . . . it stinks! For decades women have been underestimated as business leaders because of antiquated stereotypes about our attitude.

Ladies, it is time we *changed that perception.*

In business, being a class act never hurts. Never! You can be assertive without being aggressive, passionate without being pushy, and commanding without being conceited. Likewise, you can express your insight without insult, critique without criticizing, and demand without demeaning. I think, well . . . I *know* it can be a hard balance to find for many women.

As my mother always said, your exit will be remembered longer than your entrance. It is important to adjust (and sometimes re-adjust) our attitude so that it is in line with our short-term and long-term objectives. Our objectives *should* be to get the best out of life, the best out of ourselves, and the best out of others.

Attitude, when coupled with hard work, makes that possible. We cannot control most of what happens in life. We can control only ourselves, our disposition, our reactions, and our attitude. Where you go in life—along with when and how you get there—will largely be determined by attitude.

In business, attitude will always increase or decrease our odds of success. Having a can-do, must-do, will-do attitude will win business and close deals.

> *Being powerful is like being a lady. If you have*
> *to tell people you are, you aren't.*
> —Margaret Thatcher

Class Factor™: The Four Dynamics of Attitude

Your attitude is the product of four elements: How you THINK, how you SPEAK, how you ACT, and the way in which you RESPOND. The sum total of those four elements is called your *Class Factor™*. Figure 2.1 illustrates these elements.

CLASS FACTOR NUMBER ONE: *THINK*

You are what you think. What you think about yourself determines how you present yourself. It determines whether you have a positive or negative outlook on life and others. It determines whether you prepare and how others perceive you. It is the starting point for all success. So, my point, ladies, is that what you think matters. If you think that you won't be taken seriously because you're a woman, then you're right. You won't.

Whether you think you can, or think you can't, you're always right.

Many people ask me how I've been able to handle being a single and attractive woman in the world of professional sports. Isn't it intimidating? Not for me. I don't approach being a woman in business any differently than a man approaches being a man in business. I know I am just as capable as any other person who walks in the room.

Cathy Black and Bill Gates had to start somewhere. Home Depot didn't start with several thousand stores. Coca-Cola didn't start with

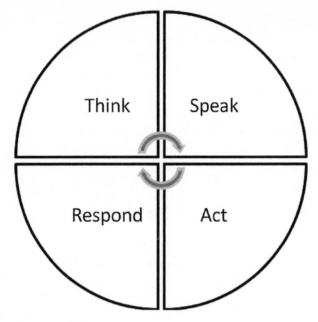

FIGURE 2.1   Class Factor™ Chart

multiple flavors. Disneyland was a dream before it became a destination. Everything great starts with a thought. As women, I believe that we fail to appreciate the importance of our thinking. As I've said before, it is important to believe in yourself and your ability to make things happen. With fearless determination and an optimistic outlook, nothing is impossible.

Conversely, it is important to be aware of the snowball effect of your thinking. If you think you can't, then you're right. You can't. If you wake up in the morning and the first thought you have is that your day will be full of challenges and negative outcomes, then, once again, you're right. If you assume that your coworker is going to give you a hard time, they probably will. If you assume that others will discount your opinion because you're a woman, or you're too young, or for any other reason, guess what? You're right again.

The sad part is that you can waste a lot of unnecessary energy with negative thinking and worrying about things that haven't even happened yet. My philosophy is: Control what you can control, do your best to impact your circumstances, but above all else, don't worry.

When you worry, you create stress. Stress has very basic and recognizable physical responses in our bodies; our stomachs clench, hormones are released, muscles tighten, and our heart rate increases. Cave women recognized these responses as meaning fight or flight; it meant a wooly mammoth or saber tooth tiger was about to strike. These days we don't have those kinds of stressors in our life. Instead of wooly mammoths, we have grumpy bosses, irritating coworkers, undermining colleagues, and less than stellar CEOs; instead of saber tooth tigers we have deadlines, paper jams, repetitive workplace injuries, and vending machine lunches.

Yet the fight or flight syndrome is still there; every time a client leaves a cryptic message—"Marshawn, call me; it's urgent!"—my body immediately goes into fight or flight and my stress and worry levels go off the charts. A million thoughts—all negative—spin through my brain: "He's firing me, I just know it. He went with someone else, I'm just sure of it. I was too aggressive; I wasn't aggressive enough . . . " On and on it goes.

What is the price of this daily—and usually multiple-times daily— physical and emotional response to worry, fear and stress? According to the CDC, "Short-lived or infrequent episodes of stress pose little risk. But when stressful situations go unresolved, the body is kept in a constant state of activation, which increases the rate of wear and tear to biological systems. Ultimately, fatigue or damage results, and the ability of the body to repair and defend itself can become seriously compromised."

When I first started EDGE 3M Sports & Entertainment, I had three nonpaying clients. I was working for three NFL athletes for free. I did this so that I could gain experience, develop my contacts, and build a foundation. After four months of no revenue, I began to get discouraged about whether things were ever going to change. Would I ever make any money?

At first, I was extremely optimistic about my ability to get endorsement deals for each of these players. I just assumed that it would be easy. Such was not the case. NFL players are much harder to market than basketball players. A football player wears a helmet, and not everyone immediately recognizes his face. I remember calling the headquarters of

Pepsico. I wanted to propose an endorsement to Mountain Dew. I called and called and called. I left messages, e-mails, and voice mails. I was determined. Then, I finally got a response. The response was thanks, but no thanks.

I admit, thoughts of giving up were heavy on my mind. But then I stepped back and realized I needed to view the negative events with a more positive outlook. I had to recognize the power and strength of these clients and get them deals based on their strengths, not their weaknesses. I looked at each one specifically, did a strengths-versus-weakness comparison, and redesigned tailor-made action plans for each one. It wasn't easy, but eventually each one got endorsement deals based on their own merits.

Your thinking (like your confidence) is magnetic. What you think determines what you attract—good or bad. Your thinking will impact the type of energy that you project. In business, thinking that you can win a deal or close a client is 80 percent of the battle, maybe even 90 percent. There is no accounting for the overwhelming impressions of confidence, poise, and positive thought. Customers, clients, and coworkers will respond to what you think and project. If you walk in the door with an optimistic outlook, you increase the odds of positive outcomes.

Class Factor Number Two: *Speak*

What you think determines how you speak; it comes down to cause and effect. If you are truly a positive person, then it will show in your conversations with others. The effect of what you think is cumulative; it deposits itself in every aspect of your personality. Whether it's the way you walk, smile, nod your head instead of shake it, instinctively reach out to shake hands with someone or even embrace them, positivity can't hide. Neither, of course, can negativity.

Have you ever met someone who has something negative to say about everyone and everything? They always see the glass as half empty, they always think there is a conspiracy, and they always expect the worst. You know what that person thinks because of what they say and how they say it. You can literally feel negativity coming off them in waves; it permeates the way they shuffle instead of bound, grimace instead of smile, slump instead of sit up. Ask yourself: Is this the image I want to portray?

As women, we should make positive declarations about ourselves and our circumstances. I truly believe that there is power in what you say. If you say to yourself, "I can close this deal. I can ace this interview. I can face my boss," then you've infinitely increased your odds of success. Likewise, when you speak positively with others, then you increase their odds of successful outcomes along with their positive perception of you.

Much of what I do at ME Unlimited is about encouraging people to live their best lives. Our company slogan is "Equipping the Motivated to LIVE out Loud." The key to being an effective motivator is authenticity. I have to believe that anything is possible if I'm going to effectively tell someone else that they can accomplish their dreams. In doing executive coaching sessions, I spend a great deal of time helping people see that one of their roadblocks to success is their speech. This is exactly what we do for thousands of women at the S.K.I.R.T.S. in the Boardroom: Set No Limits Summit as well. Because many people doubt themselves and their circumstances, they manifest that doubt in how they speak. Remember, most people know only what you tell them. If you communicate doubt and hesitation, then don't expect others to believe in you.

When I decided I wanted to start working with athletes, I did not have any professional sports clients. I was still an associate at a law firm and had no idea how to make the transition into sports. One day, I missed a flight from Atlanta to Dallas. The flight had been cancelled.

While I waited for the next flight, the person next to me asked me about my profession. I actually didn't say I was an attorney right away. I said that I owned a communication consulting company called Communication Counts (which I did), working with athletes, entertainers, and personalities. He then said that he was a sports agent and would probably have some clients for me. That's how my sports agency came into being—with my words. Someone gave me a chance because of something I said. Your success will start with what you say. Someone is *always* listening. Consider your words an invitation for others to believe in and invest in you.

Class Factor Number Three: Act

What you think has an impact on how you speak. What you say has an impact on how you act. People might hear what you say, but they will remember you for what you do. How you carry yourself is a significant component of your attitude. I believe that much of my success is due in large part to my demeanor—especially for someone under the age of 30. I carry myself with confidence and class. I underpromise and overdeliver. I work to exceed expectations. That's my trademark. We'll explore more about action in Part Two. For now, it is important to understand that the old adage is true: Actions *do* speak louder than words. Your words might get you in the door, but your actions will keep you there.

In fact, your actions communicate your level of seriousness and your dedication to your profession. For example, I was having trouble with an employee's ability to complete projects in a timely manner. On one occasion, I tasked the employee with redoing the content for our company web site. I stated what I wanted done and when I needed it. Then I expected the person to complete it.

I do not believe in micromanaging others by constantly checking in, because I hate being micromanaged myself. However, when I asked for the end product to be completed, it was not ready. That doesn't fly with me. My natural reaction was frustration. However, I chose not to address the situation right away because I knew I was frustrated. I wanted to communicate without emotion. As I stepped back, I thought about what I wanted to communicate. I set a time for a meeting about the employee's performance. This is how the conversation went.

> First, I know I expect a lot. I expect things to be done with excellence. And I know that that is a very high standard. But I refuse to accept the notion that you can't meet and exceed that standard. This is my company, but I want you to take ownership over your work. Your work matters to me. It matters to our clients. Deadlines matter as well. We can't function efficiently unless our clients can rely on us. I'm only as strong as my team. I need to be able to rely on you. I'm going to give you one more day to complete this project. I don't expect you to miss deadlines without giving me a heads-up first.

You can ask me anything, anytime you want. But the one thing I will not allow in this agency is mediocrity and apathy. No one will slow us down and remain on the team. I ask for one thing—performance. I think you can move us forward. It's not just about the web site. It's deeper than that. It's about your attitude and your approach to your work. I could be wrong, but I need you to prove me wrong. I want you to see yourself as a key piece in our company's puzzle. We need you.

The next morning, I walked into my office and the project was done before I arrived. I gained a greater appreciation for this employee because of that person's actions. Not their promises. We don't generate revenue based on promises. We can only grow as a company if our promises are grounded in commitment and action. As an individual, your success works the same way. What you do and how you do it matters.

CLASS FACTOR NUMBER FOUR: *RESPOND*

In business, we cannot control most of what happens to us. Successful companies and successful women are defined by how they react and respond to adversity and pressure. You will be evaluated not by the problems you face, but by how you face them. This is particularly challenging for women.

We are already fighting stereotypes and antiquated perceptions about our level of intelligence, capacity, and ability. This makes us question how we should respond to others. If I am *too* reserved, I won't be heard. If I am *too* vocal, I'll be perceived as difficult. If I question something because it doesn't feel right, I'll be stereotyped as indecisive.

I'm sure you have wrestled with each of these issues before—perhaps daily. The reality is that women *are* held to a higher standard—sometimes a double standard—with respect to our behavior, approach, and demeanor. That is not really going to change. So, how do we handle it? As a woman you should not be afraid to ask for what you want. And, you should not be shy about sharing what's on your mind. The key is to think before you respond.

Here are four tips:

First, appreciate who you are and what have to offer. This is the basis for having an optimistic approach to life.

Second, treat others with respect. Use this as the basis for all your communication and interactions with others.

Third, focus on what you think, not what you feel. Support your viewpoints with solid rationales, not emotion-driven opinions.

Fourth, deliver in a way that creates collective buy-in. Remember, when giving a gift, the packaging is just as important as the present. Think of your attitude as the package.

An Attitude Makeover

When your car is run down or underperforming, it gets a tune-up. When your hair is too long, too dull, or you're just looking worn-out, you get a makeover. Why should your mental attitude be any different? If you've been feeling less than positive these days, or if how other people react to you reflects back on some latent negativity that's been brewing, it could be time for an Attitude Makeover.

Following are some attitude enhancement tips that will help you advance your career or your business through the power of a positive attitude.

TIP NUMBER ONE: REMEMBER, IT'S NOT ABOUT YOU

Having a "serve me, it's all about me, cater to me" attitude is Mistake 101. Having a self-serving approach to life causes you to be impatient and arrogant. It's not attractive in a woman. And it doesn't help you reach your goals. You may be in business for yourself, but you will never be in business *by* yourself. Someone has to buy your service or product. Someone has to promote you or give you a chance. But no one owes you anything!

Anything worth having is worth earning. The more you adhere to an approach of giving, serving, helping, and assisting others, the more people will want to assist you in return. Without fail, every time I do something positive for someone else, I receive two to three times more benefit in return favors from that person.

When you help others, it shows your character. Wouldn't you rather do business with someone with good character and a giving heart? When you meet someone, your first question should be "how can I help you?" not "How can you help me?" You build trust by giving, not taking. So give of your time, your expertise, and your friendship. It will take you much further than expecting at the outset for others to do for you.

TIP NUMBER TWO: *SMILE*

I did an Internet image search for the word "smile." I was curious to see what popped up. One of the pictures that appeared was that of a smiling pig. Yes, a pig! It wasn't a real picture. It had been digitally enhanced and altered. But the picture grabbed me nonetheless. The ugly little pig was absolutely adorable.

Why? All because of a simple smile. A smile is infectious. It immediately breaks the ice. When balanced with a strong and confident demeanor, a smile can be your strongest, most disarming weapon. It enhances the way in which people perceive and therefore receive you, your thoughts, and your ideas.

When I was preparing for the interview portion of the Miss America competition, I used to do "mock" interviews with a preparatory panel. I was only 21 years old, but I loved discussing "heavy" issues of policy, law, health care, business . . . you name it. After the Q&A period, the panel would give me feedback.

One of the mock judges, Kevin, paused and said that my answers were very strong and complete. They were thought-provoking and showed good insight. Then he paused with a puzzled look on his face. I could tell that there was more he wanted to say. He said, "I can't quite put my finger on what's missing. Give me a second."

So he just stared at me. Talk about an awkward silence. He tilted his head to the other side, and continued to stare and analyze what was missing. "Aha!" he finally said.

Meanwhile I was thinking, "What is it already?!?"

Kevin then said, "Your answers are really smart. But, we know you're smart. We have your resume, you walk in the room with confidence, and you clearly know what you're talking about. But all of that is somewhat intimidating. It's just smart. There is no feeling."

"Feeling?" I thought. "What do you mean?" He went on to emphasize how the delivery affected the reception. People needed to "feel" what I was saying, not just hear what I was saying. I needed to soften my responses, not by the content, but visually, with a more pleasant packaging.

We will explore communication delivery dynamics and tips in the chapter on communication. However, the key thing to remember is that a smile always adds warmth. It is a bridge that connects you to others and draws others to you. The week of my actual Miss America interview, Kevin sent me a different card every day that said the same thing: "Feel." I focused on adding warmth to balance my bold communication style. The next day, I won the interview competition (and over $50,000 in scholarships) at Miss America.

I was *really* smiling now!

Tip Number Three: *Be Optimistic*

A positive attitude is a choice that will attract positive opportunity to you. Speak optimistically about opportunities. Be a visionary. See the future, not the past. Helen Keller, a woman who certainly had plenty to grumble about in her life, once said, "When one door of happiness closes, another opens; but often we look so long at the closed door that we do not see the one which has been opened for us." See the door of opportunity and open it with a smile!

I love that my clients trust me to help them dream big dreams. Recently I was sitting in a board meeting for a nonprofit that I work with. I was enthusiastically giving suggestions about how we could enhance an innovative new program that was launching in the city of Atlanta. One of the other board members said, "Wow! You think everything is possible, don't you?" Actually, I do. If we can perceive it, then why can't we achieve it? People refer to me as the everything-is-possible-person—the dreamer. That is not a bad thing.

I like that people see me as someone who dreams big and looks for ways to make dreams a reality. It brings me more business—people and companies trust my branding agency to help them dream—to think outside of the box, to take their brands and concepts to another level.

That starts with optimism. People will seek out your expertise. They will want to run things by you. They will want your opinion. I have been able to turn my opinions into a business.

TIP NUMBER FOUR: *CHOOSE BATTLES WISELY*

In order to embrace tip number four, you must go back to tip number one—remember that *it is not all about you.* I was at a meeting with a client's attorney the other day. I'm an attorney, but I was not representing the client in that capacity. I was handling the client's public relations on a very serious matter. While we were collectively reviewing a press release, my client's attorney referred to me as the client's "assistant." For whatever reason, I was insulted.

After all, I went to law school—a more prestigious one than the law school the other attorney had attended, at that! Because I was a woman, he just assumed that I was an assistant. It irked me! But I didn't react out of my frustration. I chose to let it go. I could have corrected him, but I probably would have come off as arrogant. That's a no-win situation.

It reminded me that my attitude is a choice. My attitude represents the influence that I want to have. So, how do you respond? You should remain professional and poised, yet principled and passionate. You have to be willing to get your point across and stand for what you believe in—this can be done without being condescending or arrogant.

You see, you have to ask yourself what's important. What objectives are accomplished by you putting someone else in their place? Sometimes it is necessary. I have never been afraid of a good showdown, but usually it's not necessary. Our ego can be deceiving. It makes us *think* we're in the right even when we're really in the wrong.

Did I mention that it's not all about you?

TIP NUMBER FIVE: *DRESS THE PART*

To be successful in business, you must dress with class and integrity. You don't have to have the most expensive outfit in the room, but you need to match! There is nothing wrong with having style, but make sure that your passion for fashion does not detract from your perception as an intellectual talent.

Do not be overly concerned about what others think. However, don't give others a reason to think negatively about you, either. Don't dress as if you are going to an evening social for singles when you are actually going to a professional meeting. That's not called being trendy; that can be perceived as trashy. How you dress *is* important. I work in male-dominated fields. I must be taken seriously if my business is going to be a viable entity. I want eye contact, not wandering eyes, when I'm trying to seal a deal or close a new client. I have been successful because I carry myself in a very professional manner, and I dress the part.

Give thought to what you wear. When I'm headed to a meeting with an NFL player, I have to be particularly careful about my appearance. Is my skirt too short? Is the neckline on my blouse too low? Are my pants too tight? Do I have too much make-up on? I also make sure that I monitor my demeanor. I don't want the guys thinking that I'm flirting with them, when I'm simply being polite and kind.

There is a fine line. I have to walk it every day. It does help that I'm a lawyer and I treat every client like a new case. I do my research; I know their profile before I walk into the room. I dress as though I'm headed to court. I don't take meetings late in the evening—even though my male counterparts can do so. I carry myself with respect, I have a strong demeanor, and as a result I command respect in return. And, I look the clients—even the 300-plus-pound defensive linemen—directly in the eyes.

How we dress is an external manifestation of our attitude. When you walk into a meeting looking like a class act, with a smile on your face, and intelligence to boot, then you've just garnered *all* of the attention in the room. A positive attitude will show in how you carry yourself. So walk with optimism. Image matters.

Tip Number Six: *Care*

Be concerned about what happens around you. You should care about your *work,* your *image* and *others.* One thing I absolutely cannot stand is apathy. It is wasted, unapplied intellect. You should have an opinion.

Expressing what you think and feel is how you show your value. When you care about an outcome, you cause others to have confidence in you. As a woman, you should speak up when you have a chance. Show your interest in your clients and work. In other words, be proactive, not reactive. Go-getters will always accomplish more than waiters.

TIP NUMBER SEVEN: *PROBLEM SOLVE*

People often complain that they haven't gotten quite far enough for how hard they've worked, but before we complain we have to analyze that statement. Sometimes working hard isn't enough; you have to work smart.

Working smart means solving problems, not just serving time. I have had several 9-to-5 jobs in my life, but they never added up to only 40 hours a week. Typically they were more like 50 to 60 hours, because there was always something to do before work, after work, during lunch, on the way there, or on the way home. Sometimes we confuse work with busy work. It's not about running around looking busy, it's about being productive and getting results.

People who solve problems effectively are those who are promoted. Think about it. We elect a president to solve problems. We look to a leader for direction. I hire people who are good problem solvers—people who can think independently, not simply follow directions.

One of the greatest ways you can do to add value to your company is to look for solutions and offer solutions. Always be forward thinking and try to circumvent problems before they arise. Doing so will make you the go-to person that others can rely on for positive results and answers.

TIP NUMBER EIGHT: *ASSOCIATE WISELY*

Don't waste major time with minor people. I don't like to spend time with people who always complain. I face enough challenges in the day. I like to surround myself with people who have positive energy. I choose to associate with other women—and men—who look for positive solutions to pressing problems. Looking on the bright side makes a big difference in how you approach life. I keep saying that attitude is by choice, not by chance.

Choose a circle of people who motivate you to do better. I was the only girl in my family—I have brothers and mostly male cousins. In order to play with the "big boys," I had to keep up. I was forced to step up my game, my effort, and my focus if I wanted to stay in the game—whatever it was. Think of your attitude as if you were an athlete training for competition. If you train with weak, feeble-minded, and slow competitors, you will never grow.

We are a product of our environment—we have the ability to change the environment by setting an example—but you'll never truly push yourself to be your best unless you surround yourself with other people who are motivated. So, for some of you it might be time to go on a people diet! It's time to cut out the people who feed you with negative thoughts and encourage negative habits. Keeping them in your life is counterproductive. Not everybody will understand your vision, dreams, and potential. If they don't get it, just move on. Don't get left behind because others are simply behind the curve.

Most of the things that I have wanted to do (and subsequently have done), were way outside of the norm. I am one of the least predictable women you'll ever meet. From pageants, to Georgetown law school, to a career in marketing and professional sports, I usually go against the grain. You have to act for yourself, not for others. Again, if others don't get you, you should move on.

I was told that I'd never make it to Miss America. I finished as third runner-up and won about $80,000 in scholarships. I was told that I shouldn't go to law school because my friends didn't see me as an attorney. I ended up graduating from Georgetown University Law Center—100 percent debt-free, at that. I was told by a supposed mentor at a former law firm where I worked that I was incapable of generating business—specifically that I wouldn't be able to build a sports practice because I was too young. And, even if I was able to secure the clients, I wouldn't know what to do with them because I hadn't been properly trained. I now own a very successful sports agency.

Sometimes people look at some of my successes and think that I've had it easy. That is not the case. As a woman under the age of 30 playing in male-dominated fields and highly competitive industries, I've always had to fight. I learned as a child in elementary school that people will try to make you feel inferior. It is a fact of life—a sad fact, but true nonetheless.

The sooner you accept that, learn how to process it (usually by ignoring it), and move on, the sooner you'll begin to see the greatness unfold in your life. People are human. They make mistakes. They will misjudge you and underestimate you (yet another fact of life). I have been discouraged by a few people. I have been disappointed by a lot of people. And, I've also been doubted by most people. If you allow those people to shape you, then we have a problem. Those people should never influence your perception of your potential.

Tip Number Nine: *Accept Yourself*

It wasn't until I was in my second year of law school that I truly embraced and accepted a very simple reality. The reality (an "aha" moment for me) was that I accepted the fact that I am a smart person. I mean really intelligent and bright. I am. My success hasn't been by accident. My success isn't just because I work hard. It has come mostly due to my intellect. (Before, I didn't see myself as smart.)

Yes, I graduated high school with honors, and finished college *magna cum laude* with a 3.87 GPA. And I know that I received over $200,000 in scholarships, and was named one of *Glamour* magazine's Top 10 College Women, a USA Today Academic All-American, and a prestigious Harry S. Truman Scholar. But I felt those things only came about because of hard work.

Now I've embraced my intelligence, which has taken me to another level in my personal and professional life. I emphasize this because I think that as women we constantly go through stages where we doubt ourselves, despite our successes, even, and especially, as we advance in our careers and new opportunities present new challenges in uncharted waters.

Don't be afraid to be smart. Accept that you are a force with which to reckoned.

Tip Number Ten: *Show Respect*

When you respect others, others respect you. This principle alone will enable you to advance in your career. If people respect you, they will grow to trust you. Carry yourself with respect and integrity. Require that men respect you. In order to do so, you have to respect yourself. You do that by acting with respect and integrity. Give careful thought and attention to what you say and how you say it.

With my pro athlete clients, I make a special effort to set the stage and explain to my clients what my expectations are for our working relationship. I sit every new client down and tell him two things: "First, I need and require honesty. Second, I need and require responsiveness. If something happens, tell me. If I call you, respond right away. This job isn't a game for me. You're entrusting me with a piece of your life. My only concern is operating in your best interest. That is my only priority. As a result, I will not always tell you what you want to hear. I will tell you what you need to hear. That is my promise to you. So, in order for me to do my job for you, I need honesty and responsiveness. If you respect my time and energy, we'll be able to work together to make history and create a long-lasting legacy."

Then I ask the client what their expectations are. Usually they are stunned that I did this in the first place. When you start relationships by setting expectations, you create a dynamic of mutual respect. Speak up to get respect. State what you want and what you expect. Carry yourself with confidence, class, integrity, and compassion. It's that simple. Men will respect you. Women will as well. They may be intimidated by you, but that's not your concern. You can't live beneath your potential because others fear just how fierce and dynamic you are. Not your problem!

Tip Number Eleven: *Appreciate*

Much of what we think we have would cease to exist if we learned to appreciate what we actually have. Furthermore, in business, appreciate the little things that your clients and customers do, and do not take people or opportunity for granted.

If your client calls you back, thank them for getting back to you. Believe me, not everyone returns phone calls. If your employee delivers a project on time, praise and support them for their efforts and their work. That will continue to motive them to perform with excellence. I make a conscious effort to say two short words that go a long way: "Thank you." Sometimes, that is all people need and want to hear.

Tip Number Twelve: *Envy Not*

One of the biggest challenges that we have as women is working together without jealousy. When I was on the television show *The*

Apprentice, Donald Trump divided our teams into men versus women. The women's team consistently lost. The only week that we won a task as an all-woman's team was the week that I was project manager.

We lost every other task. The men's team, on the other hand, kept winning. They had an excellent, supportive team dynamic. Eventually, the women lost so many team members to boardroom firings that Mr. Trump had to send a few men to play on our team. That was embarrassing! The team kept losing because the women wouldn't get along. It seemed to me that they were jealous and bickering over things that did not really matter.

Who cares if someone is wearing a designer suit with killer pumps? Don't talk behind her back—instead, give her a compliment. Envy and jealousy will always break up a team, and it will impact your ability to focus on what really matters most. As women, we should support each other.

I recognize that envy is a very human emotion; it's in our nature to resent those who have more than us and covet what they have, whether those assets are real or perceived. It's why we love gossip sites so much; we can hack on this star's cellulite or how that one looks without make-up. But here's the thing about envy: It hurts you more than it hurts them.

Envy slows you down and wears you out. It's off-task and off-target; it's empty calories in the banquet of life. Envy is perhaps one of the least productive human emotions on the planet, and possibly the least effective job skill you'll ever have. Whenever you feel the urge to envy, remember to appreciate what you have. It will actually give you a professional advantage because you remain focused and undistracted by things you cannot control.

Your Attitude Quotient:
Three Factors and How They Affect You

In the final analysis, what *is* attitude?

In a word, it's everything; but what is it made of? We all know the sum of our parts creates the whole, but breaking down those parts in search of something as far-reaching and enigmatic as attitude can be challenging.

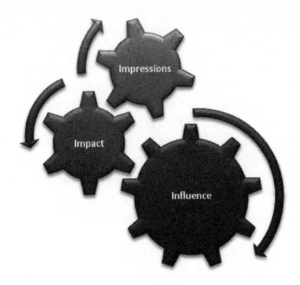

F<small>IGURE</small> **2.2** Impressions, Impact, and Influence

Have no fear; Attorney Acronym (as the head of my management team, Raoul Davis, calls me) is here to the rescue. When you break it down, attitude is really a series of *impressions,* which determine your *influence.* Your influence, in turn, determines your *impact.* Figure 2.2 shows how all three aspects of your attitude are interrelated.

- ◆ **Impressions:** Your attitude does not live in a vacuum; it emanates from within, envelopes you in a certain way, and, in many cases, proceeds you wherever you go. We all make impressions; good, bad or ugly. What's important to remember is that you get to choose which impression you make. For instance, you walk into a room. What do people do? Do they sit up and take notice, smile in recognition and warmth, embrace you with their body language, and welcome you before even meeting you? That's one impression. Or do they cringe, smirk, roll their eyes, stiffen, and blanche to see you coming? That's another impression.

- ◆ **Influence:** Your impressions have influence over your life and the lives of others. In business, even when we are at the top, we're all part of a team. The impression you make can literally influence the success of a sale, a campaign, getting or losing a client, or winning or losing a big bid. If you walk into that room with a negative attitude, like a virus it will eventually infect the entire room. But if you walk in positively, capably, forcefully, and ready to enthuse the troops with your positive attitude, you build up the group's immunity to negativity; your influence over them becomes a positive one that you can all share.

♦ **Impact:** Impressions lead to influences, influences lead to impact. What impact can your influence have over a meeting, a conference call, an interview, or a presentation? There is the immediate impact you make with your presence, the intermediate impact you make with your attitude, and the lasting impact you make with your actions (which are, of course, based on your attitude). Think of impact as your legacy. What kind will you leave?

Three Attitude Types: *Which One Are You?*

The great thing about attitude is that it's a symptom, not a disease. In other words, it's an adjective, not a noun; it describes how you act, it doesn't determine who you are. You can change your attitude. Why? Because it comes from within, and it's based on choice. You determine your attitude with the way you look at the world, and the way you look at the world comes from how you deal with positive or negative emotions.

Simply knowing that you can change your attitude is one step toward—guess what—changing your attitude. But first you need to identify where you fall on the attitude scale. So now that we know the importance and value of attitude, let's turn our attention to identifying which kind of attitude you have.

There are three basic attitude types (see Figure 2.3).

1. Observer (neutral): The observer watches from the sidelines, too doubtful to set foot on the playing field or, if called into action, too timid to make much of an impact. This is a safe attitude; it risks little and affects few. While the observer's performance may be "adequate," it will always border on mediocre because observers rarely get the kind of aggressive, creative, outside-of-the-box results that modern companies thrive on today.

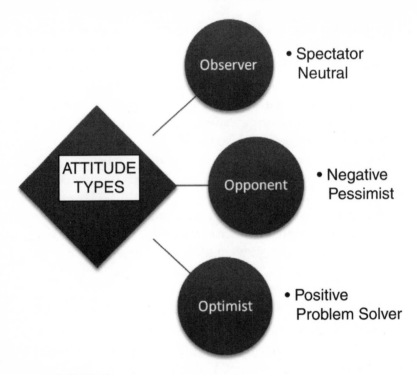

FIGURE 2.3   Attitude Types

2. *Opponent (negative):* Unlike the observer, the opponent isn't passive; she is actually active. She may be on a team, but she challenges the team—and not in a good way. She becomes the opponent wherever she goes, consistently criticizing every aspect of the organization and grumbling about how she can do things better, but never actually getting around to doing them. If we look at the impression-influence-impact flow chart from the last section, the critic makes a bad impression, subjects everyone to a negative influence, and has an impact that can be company-wide if left unchecked.

3. *Optimist (positive):* The optimist is the S.K.I.R.T. companies are looking for to hire, promote, and lead them: optimistic, positive, and creating a strong impression wherever she (or he) may go. In fact, optimism is usually the one common denominator linking all successful female business owners and entrepreneurs. Positive

people breed positivity; they not only inject a much-needed dose of optimism into an organization, but they infect that organization with resilience to negativity along the way. The optimist is a problem solver who makes firm decisions, and lots of them, out of a seat of positive energy that recognizes failure and error as part of the cost of doing business today, but not the reason for making negative decisions.

Aptitude for Attitude

As we have seen, attitude is a learned behavior; it may be something we're inclined to have, but we're not born with our attitude fully formed. Sure, there are kids who seem to come out of the womb quiet, introverted, and doubtful, just as there are bouncing babies who are positive, giggling, and ebullient.

But just as we are born, grow up, educate ourselves, assert our independence, and move away from home and change our address, so can we question, understand, identify, and change our attitude. Class is about having an attitude that says, "I am positive, unfailing, dignified, and true; I care about myself to *be* my very best; I care enough about you to *give* my very best."

Anne Frank once famously said, "Then, without realizing it, you try to improve yourself at the start of each new day; of course, you achieve quite a lot in the course of time. Anyone can do this; it costs nothing and is certainly very helpful. Whoever doesn't know it must learn and find by experience that a quiet conscience makes one strong."

Know yourself and respect yourself enough to embrace a more positive and optimistic attitude. Know what works; avoid what doesn't. When people complain to me that "It's not just as simple as turning a frown upside down," surprise them by readily agreeing. I know as well as anybody that it takes time, patience, and "a quiet conscience" to create a stronger, more positive attitude. But I always reply, "Look, you've lived your life for 30, 40, or 50 years doubting yourself, worrying over nothing, and borrowing trouble. Where has it gotten you? What do you have to lose by spending the next 30, 40, or 50 years doing the exact opposite and being positive and optimistic?" If I do say so myself, it's a pretty valid argument.

The best part about creating a positive attitude is that how you spend the rest of your years is entirely up to you!

Set No Limits Reflection

As women, we have to be in control of our emotions and understand what factors influence our behavior. If knowledge is power, then knowing yourself will absolutely empower you. Nobody is perfect. Everyone has a negative trigger.

ATTITUDE TRIGGERS: WHAT IS HOLDING YOU BACK?

Negative triggers are usually associated with something internal going on with ourselves. Or your triggers may be associated with something external with other people or circumstances. Take some time to identify which factors cause you to have a negative or unproductive attitude.

WHICH FACTORS CAUSE ME TO HAVE A BAD ATTITUDE?

Internal Factors

Stress   Insecurity   Pressure   Fatigue   Hunger   Confusion

External Factors

Negative People   Intimidating Situations   Time Pressure

How can I address each of these factors?

_____

_____

_____

_____

_____

Your attitude and your response to adversity is a choice. You can learn more about Class Factors, Attitude Types, and personal triggers at www.skirtsintheboardroom.com. Take the time to understand what causes you to act and react in a less than productive manner so you can recognize these triggers before they take over.

Chapter 3

Course

Women Are Better Drivers

> **Course (*n*) Onward movement in a particular direction; progress.**

Why is it that women are usually willing to ask for directions when lost, but men refuse? Some think it is because women are more sensible and less stubborn. I think it is because our desire to reach our destination is stronger. We have a purpose in mind.

It is virtually impossible to define who you are and where you are going without having a clear understanding of your purpose. Possessing a sense of purpose is essential. It helps us to deal with difficult personalities, take risks, make tough financial decisions, and create new opportunities that will enrich our personal and professional destiny.

A sense of purpose empowers us to resist mediocrity, and equips us to persevere through adversity. Purpose is your reason, your function, and your intention. It gives you meaning and shapes your goals. Purpose both propels you and protects you. In essence, having a strong sense of purpose serves three vital functions. It becomes your (1) compass, (2) conviction, and (3) courage.

Function One: *Compass*

Purpose guides us. It's like having a roadmap leading you to your destination and your destiny. Further, like a compass, it lets you know when you are on the right path. But first, you have to know how to use it.

I went on a boating scavenger-hunt with a group of lawyers one summer—we were actually competing against other teams of lawyers. I know: You would think lawyers have a better way to utilize their time!

I had never been boating in my life and it sounded like fun until we got to the lake. It was huge! We had a map, but it was not enough. The map would have been fine if we had a bird's-eye view, but we were *in* the water, not over it. Looking out from the boat, it was hard to determine where we were, must less where we needed to go. We had a full tank of gas and a complete crew aboard, but we could not go anywhere.

We had no true sense of direction. Then, it dawned on someone to look for a compass. I opened the box of gadgets and, voilà, we had one! Thank goodness. Now, the next challenge was to figure out how to use it. Only one person knew how. We completely relied upon that little needle to lead us from island to island. In the end, our team won the competition—a team of first-time sailors! The difference was not the fact that we had a compass in our possession. After all, each of the teams had one. *The difference was our ability to use it effectively.*

The same holds true with purpose. The goal is not learning to possess purpose. All of us were born with it. The goal is to find it, use it and rely on it. Up until this point, you may not have truly believed that purpose is something that has always lived inside of you, but it does. My team in the previous example did not even know we had the compass in our arsenal. Discovering its existence was only step one. You see, step one requires you to acknowledge and embrace the fact that you were created on purpose and with purpose. Step two requires you to unlock it and utilize it.

> *Alice came to the fork in the road.*
> *"Which road do I take?" she asked.*
> *"Where do you want to go?" responded the Cheshire cat.*
> *"I don't know," Alice answered.*
> *"Then," said the cat, "it doesn't matter."*
> —Lewis Carroll, *Alice in Wonderland*

PURPOSE-DRIVEN ASSETS

Purpose is a vital business asset. It will distinguish you from your competition, and it will enable you to find your way when others cannot.

In the boating story, my entire team had to rely upon the person who knew how to use the compass. He (yes, it was a man) was the only person who could give the team guidance. *His* sense of direction gave *our* team direction. More importantly, his sense of direction gave us the confidence to trust him. The lesson to be learned here is that possessing a strong sense of direction and a clear vision *will* add value to you and your career.

In my business, the world of professional sports and brand marketing, having a clear vision is key to sustaining a strong client base. My agency's sole objective is to build iconic brands. You cannot build without a blueprint—especially when building something as abstract as branding. Most of my clients choose to hire us before the "building" goes up. They hire us based on our vision for taking them to the next level. The same is true in sales, the legal profession, real estate, financial services, consulting, and you name it. People will value your skill and expertise *more* when you are driven by purpose. They will begin to see you as a value-add to their business because they will begin to see you as the missing link in the bridge connecting them to progress and advancement. The truth is we all want to be connected to people who are problem solvers. During an election, we look for the person best suited to solve the problems affecting our communities. During turbulent times at a company, the board of directors will look for the executive who is most qualified to take the company to the next level. How? By solving its problems. My clients—every single one of them—rely on my vision and sense of direction. My purpose is helping others maximize their potential. I know that. I embrace it, and it serves as the foundation for all of my business properties. It is the filter by which I hire employees and choose which projects our agency will accept. Knowing my purpose—as the leader of my company—is what has enabled extraordinary growth in a short period of time. It has enabled my team and my clients to trust me.

Likewise, a strong sense of direction will cause clients and colleagues to trust you, and then follow you. It will also enable you to take leadership roles on special projects. Your boss will come to you for insight and strategic advice. There is no substitute for good direction. Anyone who has ever followed the wrong person, ended up in the wrong place, or received terrible advice knows that bad directions take you in only one direction—and that's off course.

Success is simply an external manifestation of your purpose-driven vision in action.

TEAM BUILDING

Direction also serves as a confidence builder. Again, in the boating example above, the man with the compass was confident because he *knew* where he was going. As a result, his confidence—directly caused by his sense of direction—inspired confidence in the rest of the team. He could not have won the scavenger hunt by himself.

He needed the rest of the team to know that the destination was attainable. We needed to understand the vision and the plan for getting there. Once we saw it, we could then seek it. We became motivated to work together to reach our goal with energy and enthusiasm. *Good direction is contagious.* Everyone wants it because direction helps us know where—and how—to take the next step. Now others have a reason to work hard and to persevere. When I meet a client who has a strong sense of vision for where they want to take their company or themselves, it motivates our team to work that much harder to make the client's vision a reality.

The same principles can be applied to building confidence and fostering cohesive teams in the workplace or in your company. If you have ever—or ever have to—manage people, having a sense of direction will determine the effectiveness of your leadership. Direction is like a flashlight that leads you.

If you want others to be on the same page, it is necessary that they understand and embrace your objective. If you have a strong sense of direction and can communicate it with assurance and clarity, then you pass the torch to others.

Regardless of whether you work for someone or if you are in business for yourself, you are never in business *by* yourself. In one way or another, you will need other people to help you realize your vision, dreams, and goals.

You will need investors to understand your direction if you want them to invest in your company. You will need employees to understand your direction if you want them to be equipped to do their jobs effectively and with enthusiasm. You will need consumers to understand your direction if you expect them to buy your products or services.

You will need to make sure that your management team—those charged with facilitating day-to-day operations—understands your direction if you expect them to make decisions that benefit your company and you. It is also key that others understand your direction if you ever expect to retire!

Your direction influences more than you realize.

DISCERNMENT

Just as I did not get a bird's-eye view of the lake that day, we do not get a bird's-eye view of life. We go through this journey step by step. Experience helps. Education helps. However, each can go only so far. If you stop to think about it, experience and education are meaningless if you are not aligned with your purpose.

An educated and experienced pilot without a flight plan is useless. The biggest asset we have, particularly as women, is an internal compass that guides our footsteps. I also call it discernment or intuition. Discernment is what shapes our judgment, acumen, insight, perceptiveness, acuity, wisdom, and choices. It is your sensitivity to you; your willingness to listen to your inner self. No recipe for success can be complete without it. Intuition is the needle in your compass. Your purpose is what guides it.

Finally, I must warn you to be aware of "magnetic deviations." Magnetic deviations are objects that can disturb the arrow on a compass because of an intervening magnetic attraction—perhaps a staple, magnetic fragments in the soil, or anything carrying iron. (I guess I remember a little bit from physics!) Magnetic attractions are not always visible, but they exist nonetheless. As you might guess, a magnetic deviation is dangerous because it can misalign your compass. You might actually *think* you are going in the right direction, but your compass is broken. You are following a deviated needle.

From time to time, we all have distractions that take us outside our purpose. We listen to other people and ignore our intuition. God gives us dreams and ideas that reveal our purpose and direction. By refusing to listen, we put ourselves on the wrong course. Often, listening to others can cause you to be on someone else's track pursuing someone else's dream. It is the equivalent of a magnetic deviation. The effect is that you *think* you are going in the right direction, but have no clue that you are already lost.

Quick Tip
Choose to read your compass correctly (going where the needle points), not conveniently (pointing the needle in the direction you think is best).

Extremely successful women—Martha Stewart, Oprah, and eBay's Meg Whitman, among others—have impeccable discernment. A gut instinct. An inkling. A hunch. That small, still voice that only you hear. It is that out-of-the-blue instinct you get to turn left instead of right. That feeling you label as an unexplainable something.

You know, when you say, "*Something* told me to go back, or *something* just told me to go." That something is more than a something. It is your compass. It is your internal navigation system, specifically and divinely designed to give you direction in every area of your life, including business.

Most successful business deals transpire because someone followed their intuition. If you recall in the introduction, I mentioned that many are called, but few are chosen. The difference between the "called" and the "chosen" is that the chosen choose to answer. Answering is the equivalent of listening to and following that voice.

In order to do so, two things are required. First, you must embrace the fact that your intuition is real. It is God's way of speaking to you and guiding you. It is a gift given to every person, but I believe the volume of the voice is particularly amplified for women. Second, you must put yourself in a position to actually hear. That means you need to make quiet time. You can take quiet time anywhere, *but you have to take it for it to be truly effective.*

Quick Tip
Learning to listen to yourself will strengthen your ability to follow your intuition.

In the hustle and bustle of balancing business and home life, women usually neglect themselves. They cut out "me" time in order to make time for everybody and everything else in their lives. Time to reflect, refresh, renew, and rest is not a luxury if you want to succeed; it is mandatory.

It is only during that quiet, reflective time that you turn down the volume of life and get to listen to your innermost thoughts and feelings again—to reconnect with the reasons you became so busy in the first place. For a few moments, you turn off complaints, demands, and deadlines. I liken it to getting into the office super-early. No one is around, and it is remarkably quiet and peaceful. No secretaries, no bosses, no co-workers. Just you at your desk. What is really remarkable is how much work you are able to accomplish in that environment. Same office, same desk, same to-do list, yet *different climate and very different results.*

You are more focused during that quiet work time, and you have a chance to shape your schedule for the day. It gives you more focus and direction to deal with all of the "noise" that is now only moments away from arrival. Starting your day with focus helps you keep focused for the remainder of the day.

QUICK TIPS: LEARNING TO LISTEN

For many of us, listening to ourselves is a skill to be learned rather than a habit we have already acquired. This is due to environment. In the hurly-burly world of high-stakes, fast-paced business dealings, it can often feel as if you need to talk twice as fast just to keep up. Unfortunately, when the workday is done, we are still operating in catch-up mode and think that listening to ourselves is a luxury, not a necessity. But, as in most things, it is quality, not quantity, that counts when it comes to listening—particularly when it comes to listening to your own inner voice.

As Albert Einstein once said, "The monotony and solitude of a quiet life stimulates the creative mind." Think about it. Where do you have your best ideas and most inspiring thoughts? In the shower? In the bathroom? (Don't be embarrassed—it's just girl talk!) If you are a driven woman with big dreams, the challenge for you is the same challenge I deal with every day—taking quality "me" time.

I was in law school at Georgetown when I bought my first home in Atlanta. At age 25, I was extremely excited to become a homeowner after 20 years of schooling (starting with kindergarten). One of the big selling points was the huge bathtub in the master bedroom. So, I moved into the house. Two years passed by, and guess what? I used the bathtub only two times in two years! Instead, I would always choose to use the shower. It was, and still is, the quickest option. With a shower, I have instant water and maybe eight seconds to wait before the water is hot and ready for business! However, my bathtub is on the third floor, so I have to wait longer for the water to get hot and then I have wait for the tub to fill up. It is a longer wait, which requires more patience and preplanning. I have to budget my time better to allow for the water to heat up and fill up. But I made a resolution to myself to use that time as "me" time. And it has been worth it. I actually had a revelation one day. The word B.A.T.H. is an acronym for *Being Able to Hear*. I had so many things going on in my day that it was hard for me to wind down and sleep. Without sleep, I was restless and less effective during the next day, which produced a never-ending cycle of restlessness and added stress. By taking the time to start or end my day with a B.A.T.H., I'm able to hear, focus, and relax. In turn, it makes me more alert, more productive, and even more innovative.

We've dedicated an entire session at the S.K.I.R.T.S. in the Boardroom: Set No Limits Summit to helping women find balance and harmony in their personal and professional life. We have some great tips for you at www.skirtsintheboardroom.com. Following the few quick tips that are listed here will help you listen better, and ease you into that quiet place where you can be your most creative and complete in order to take back control of your day.

◆ *Change this one habit today:* Distractions are the building blocks of unnecessary noise. If you're seeking for more quiet time but don't know where to find it, look at your life as a stranger might and see it for the first time. For instance, we often spend a good chunk of our day in our car—driving to and from work, the long commute, running errands, and so on. This can be valuable time for rest and reflection or wasted time spent on noisy distractions that add little and take much. Turn off music in your car when you are driving alone. Use that time as a chance to think and reflect.

◆ *Prioritize for peacefulness:* Find a quiet place in your home *and* in your office where you can go to clear your mind. Maybe you can find it under your desk, by closing your door, or in a stall in the bathroom. Just make it a priority to find a place and go to it for refuge.

◆ *Build reflection time into your schedule:* Schedule "me" time in the morning, during the day, or in the evening. It does not have to be long, but it should be long enough to help you re-center.

◆ *Breathe and stretch:* Breathing is underrated; many researchers and quite a few religions focus on breathing as a way to reach inner peace by controlling our outer actions. Stopping to take deep breaths helps you to relax, release tension, and gather your thoughts. Along with breathing, taking time (I recommend at least three times a day) to stretch will also release stress and relax your muscles.

◆ *Pamper yourself:* Take time to treat yourself, for example, by going to a spa to get a massage or a manicure. Or treat yourself to a movie or a nice dinner. The important thing is that you do something you like. You will feel refreshed and refocused.

◆ *Exercise:* Exercise releases stress and it enables your mind and body to harmonize. Don't read the word *exercise* and think I mean three hours in the gym. Walking around the parking lot during your lunch break or up and down the stairs before or after work, and even yard work or cleaning out the garage, can constitute as exercise. Simply moving your body and keeping your heart pumping achieves the desired effect. And, if you have a really rough day, invest in some boxing gloves or take an aerobic kickboxing class.

The Right Race

Extraordinarily successful people understand that you cannot be all things to all people. You cannot do everything. Just because an opportunity looks goods does not mean that it is good for you. There are certain paths that you are not meant to travel. All you have is your time. You cannot get it back.

Why waste your time traveling a path meant for someone else? That is not operating with excellence. Operating outside your purpose is like running a race in the wrong lane. You may get to the finish line, but you still will not win. That's because it was never your race in the first place. Your compass, your discernment, and the guiding power of your purpose are what keep you in your lane, and help you to run the race marked just for you.

Function Two: *Conviction*

Just as purpose propels and guides us like a compass, it also protects us. I call the protective function of purpose conviction. A conviction is a strong, firmly rooted belief or value system. It's what helps you know when to say yes, when to say no, when to stay, and when to go.

I have to use my intuition in developing my client-based business. It is true—everything that glitters isn't gold. And everything that looks good might not be good. Working with celebrities and professional athletes in the NFL, NBA, WNBA, and Major League Baseball can look very glamorous from the outside. I always emphasize to my team that EDGE 3M is an agency driven by purpose, not by popularity. Sometimes we have to turn down a potential client with a multimillion-dollar deal because the client is not right for us. That's tough! If we were driven to work with athletes for the sake of working with athletes, you would see a different result. However, we are driven by the purpose of helping others to maximize their potential. Those people have to *want* to become their best self. I learned at the very beginning that I cannot protect my clients from themselves. I can give advice and counsel, but I cannot make another person's decisions for him or her. If someone—let's say a basketball player—walks through the door with an arrogant, self-centered, obnoxious, I-am-god's-gift-to-the-world attitude, he is not the right client. Why, he probably will be condescending to me and to the staff, which is something that I don't allow. He will probably skip scheduled appearances and media interviews, which damages our agency's reputation in the industry. So, even though this person might seem like an ideal client, adding them to our client roster is not worth it in the long run. They can become less of an asset and more of a liability.

Now, I don't expect every athlete to be perfect, or to have never gotten into trouble. However, they have to be focused on improving their life, giving back to the community, and positively developing their brand long-term . . . not just for more exposure and a quick endorsement. We value substance over style.

When I first started EDGE 3M, I had three clients. Well, three pseudo-clients—they weren't actually paying me anything just yet. I needed to meet more people in the world of sports. I was introduced to an athlete who had remarkable talent. But there was something that didn't sit well with me. I did not get the feeling that this guy was being honest with me about his goals and objectives. I got the feeling that he was saying what he thought I needed to hear. Two days after I spoke with my original partners about waiting and holding off, the athlete was arrested and in the middle of a negative-media avalanche.

Please understand that we will *never* shy away from a crisis management situation affecting any of our clients. However, this was not the right type of attention or the circumstances we needed to launch our business with our first major client. Yes, things happen, but this was not the right project for us at that time. If any of our clients get into a negative situation, we stick by them and develop a crisis management strategy. I'm not saying dump your client's when they're down! I am saying choose your clients—and your alliances—wisely. Conviction equips and enables you do that.

Keep in mind that saying no can be hard. We needed a major client. However, by strategically choosing our business relationships and carefully recruiting clients, we've been able to grow our business by 400 percent in less than a year and half. Allowing conviction to protect us has strengthened our reputation and enabled our growth.

In the spirit of sisterhood, my advice to you is as follows: Be willing to walk away from a deal, a client, a partnership, or an opportunity if it does not feel right, or if the person does not respect your time and expertise.

For a woman, this can be challenging. Sometimes clients want to work with you just because they want to date you. You've probably been there before, right? We all have. That can be extremely frustrating (even if he's handsome). Our agency philosophy is that you cannot lose what you were never supposed to have. Period. So, if they walk away, there are more fish in the sea and brighter stars in the sky. Doing that has enabled me to focus my energies on where I need to be—which is not always the same as where I might *think* I want to be. And, it prevents me from trying to force partnerships that will inevitably become headaches later.

People do business with people that they like. So should you. First, you have to be likeable. But next, you have to be willing to have a filter—a boundary and a process—for choosing your partnerships and alliances. This applies to business owners. And it applies to people within a company who are looking to advance. Everyone in the company cannot be your best friend. You cannot get every promotion, everyone cannot be your mentor, and you cannot be all things to all people. But, since you *do* need people to advance (either as an entrepreneur or an executive), having a value system will help you build effectively and filter properly. With a value system, you're lean and efficient.

The lesson here is that all opportunities are not created equal. Do not spend major time with minor people.

Conviction-Based Values

Conviction can be described as an A-B-C value system, as shown in Figure 3.1.

Our values shape our attitudes, beliefs, and choices. What we think, what we believe, and what we do reflects our understanding (or lack of understanding) about our purpose. Your purpose should be guarded. This means, if you are purpose-driven, you will naturally set boundaries.

Figure 3.1 Conviction: A Value System

So, essentially, beliefs and boundaries are the same thing. Because your purpose leads you to set boundaries, it protects you. Most of the problems people see in their personal and professional lives are the result of an unwillingness to set boundaries or the consequences from boundaries that are crossed.

Everyone needs boundaries. There is a good reason you are required to drive in the appropriate lane. The purpose is safety. When you cross the line, you endanger yourself and others. We have laws for a reason. Without laws, there would be no order.

In a board game, we have rules for a reason. Without rules, there is no objective in playing the game. The purpose would be lost because there would be no boundaries and no guiding principles. Boundaries are healthy; they are necessary. However, few people take the time to define their purpose. Even fewer take the time to clearly establish boundaries. You will not meet a successful person who has wandered through life without self-imposed restrictions. You have to know when to say "When."

The old adage is true. If you do not stand for something, you will fall for anything. Purpose gives us something for which to stand. As a result, we naturally eliminate anything inconsistent with our purpose. It is what teaches us when to say "When." It is like a filter that helps us sift through the good and the bad, the necessary and unnecessary.

Your ability to sift impacts both your small and your sizeable successes. Business is about being able to differentiate the good from the bad, like picking stocks. If you can sift through all of an advisor's financial fluff and pick a profitable stock, you stand to profit. It begins with setting boundaries. For example, if you sit down with a financial advisor and have a predetermined budget about how much you are willing to invest, you are walking in the door with boundaries: limits on your spending.

Now you are able to give parameters to the advisor. If you choose to invest more than you planned, you are over your budget, which can cause consequences all on its own. What is more dangerous is if you walk into the office with no budget at all. In this case, you give the financial advisor the power to set your boundaries for you. Instead, that person should be advising you within your boundaries.

If you refuse to set limitations, someone or something else will always do it for you. There will always be more hours that you can spend in the office. Clients will have no problem asking you to work around the clock and on weekends. There will always be plenty of committees in the community and at your job that simply cannot function without you. People, often unconsciously, will set your agenda for you *if* you let them.

It can happen subtly, little by little, when purpose is not guiding your choices. The agenda of others may or may not be in your best interest, *but never forget that you are the driver.* You choose the lane and the speed, and you cannot afford to fall asleep at the wheel. Your purpose and your peace of mind are too important to entrust to backseat drivers. Having a sense of purpose—an objective, a plan, and a mission— enables you to set boundaries and stay on track.

JUST SAY "NO"

Part of setting boundaries is knowing what is important to you. You must also be willing to say "no" when something is not right for you, or when it is simply too much. Many people cannot say "no." I think the can't-say-"no"-syndrome is especially true, if not problematic, for women. It is really not our fault (is it ever?). In business, we feel as though we have to prove ourselves, more so than men do. We want to prove our dedication and ability. In trying to prove ourselves, we say "yes" to everyone—and everything. That is never healthy.

I had to say to "no" to a major potential client. I even stopped pursuing the client because of how he talked to me. He was condescending and rude. His attitude became clear after I declined several invitations to dinner. As a result, I just stopped all communication with this person and moved on with other business development efforts. About two months later, the potential client came back to me and desperately wanted our agency to work with him on a major project— a deal that would generate a quarter of a million dollars for our company. This was perfect. In terms of leverage, now I was the one being recruited . . . not the other way around. I didn't have to promote the agency's services and then try negotiating for higher compensation. I was in a better position to set my terms without *any* negotiation.

I honestly did not care whether he would hire us. I explained to him the reasons why we had stopped recruiting him the first time around. And, lo and behold, this chauvinistic male with regular displays of jerklike tendencies *apologized*. Hallelujah! I never saw that one coming. I told him that we appreciated his invitation, and that we would consider his offer to retain our agency. Of course, he would have to pay to play. I told him our price tag, take it or leave it. Now, that doesn't always work, but in this scenario it did. We gained a great client and established a great working relationship. I believe it's because we were able to set clear boundaries and firm expectations. Sometimes—especially for women— you have to draw a line in the sand, based on your convictions, and refuse to budge. And sometimes it pays off.

DELEGATE, DELEGATE, DELEGATE

Delegation is protection. It protects you from burnout. Learning to delegate and communicate when you need help is not a sign of weakness. If you do so responsibly, it shows that you have keen perception. Working hard and working smart can be as different as night and day. Working smart is not about doing it all. It is about doing all *you* should do. Doing work better left to someone else reduces efficiency.

In fact, one of the best decisions I made was hiring the head of my management team, Raoul Davis, and his company, Ascendant Strategy Group (ASG), to manage my speaking engagements with ME Unlimited. ASG specializes in working with CEOs who live a hectic lifestyle. They've helped me to lessen my hands-on workload, become better organized, and develop new concepts that enable me to continually reinvent myself. The funny part is that the same thing that I do in managing my sports and celebrity clients, ASG does for me! So, I should be able to manage myself better, right? Nope! One thing you learn as a lawyer is that you should never represent yourself. You should never do everything yourself if you can avoid it. Finding people whom you can trust will help you to be more efficient and productive.

Of course, sometimes you have to pick up the slack, work on weekends, and burn the midnight oil. However, those times should be phases in your career, not to be expected daily by everyone, including yourself. Phases are meant to end. If it never ends, it might be time to reevaluate where you are versus where you should be. Your career should bring you joy.

We cannot be all things to all people. Trust me, I know. I have been there, done that, gotten the headache, and couldn't find time to buy the T-shirt! There are many things that we could do, but very few things that we should do. Purpose helps us establish our convictions, our values, our shoulds, and our should-nots. It helps us to set priorities (to determine what is important to us) and then to prioritize (to place our priorities in proper order). Conviction will help you determine what is right and wrong for *you*. It will strengthen your compass and keep you on course. Ultimately, the function of conviction is to teach and protect us.

Quick Tip

Be willing to say "no." Make sure that "no" ends with a period, not a question mark.

Function Three: *Courage*

The final function of purpose is courage. A strong sense of purpose motivates you to step outside the box. You will never close deals if you fail to open the door in the first place. You will never win the games that you do not play. You will never make the shots that you refuse to take. Success is a product of the decisions *you* make, the risks *you* take, the network *you* generate, and the opportunities *you* create. Purpose motivates you to step on the field, a.k.a. into the boardroom. There is one common theme here: the emphasis on *you*.

Previously, I mentioned that purpose serves several functions. As our compass, it guides us and enables us to reach our goals. As our conviction, purpose protects us through a shielding system of standards and values.

Our fundamental belief system determines who we are. We are what we think. Our thoughts influence our self-image—how we see

FIGURE 3.2 Compass Needle Alignment

ourselves. Do you see yourself as a risk-taker? Our self-image influences our courage. Our courage influences the actions we take. The risks we take reflect the rewards we reap. Courage is simply the alignment of your self-image with your purpose.

> *Courage is like trying a new lipstick. You are not sure what to expect, but the reward is worth the risk.*
> —Marshawn Evans

At the end of the day, excellence requires constant, consistent, and confident steps of faith. In the same way, many are called, but few are chosen. The chosen ones are those who choose to answer. Have I mentioned this before? We will delve deeper into the concept of courage further on. For now, let's take some time to sharpen your sense of direction and align the arrow in your compass (see Figure 3.2).

Compass "Needle" Alignment

In order to make sure you are headed in the right direction, carefully answer the following questions:

NORTH
What NEW OPPORTUNITIES are Awaiting?

1. _____

2. _____

3. _____

4. _____

SOUTH
In What Areas Should I STAY PUT?

1. _____

2. _____

3. _____

4. _____

EAST
Are My EXPECTATIONS in Line with My Focus?

1. _____

2. _____

3. _____

4. _____

WEST
How am I WORKING Toward My Goals?

1. _____

2. _____

3. _____

4. _____

Lessons for M.E. (Motivation and Empowerment)

Success is a product of the decisions *you* make, the risks *you* take, the network *you* generate, and the opportunities *you* create. Being on course requires purpose. Having a sense of purpose is what guides you personally and professionally. Purpose propels you and protects you. It helps you set a course and determine where you will go and won't go. A strong sense of purpose serves three vital functions.

1. *Function One:* Purpose is your COMPASS. It gives you guidance and direction.
2. *Function Two:* Purpose is your CONVICTION. Through establishing your values and standards, it protects you from crossing boundaries.
3. *Function Three:* Purpose is your COURAGE. It drives you to strive for excellence, motivates you to dream, and enables you to take risks.

Set No Limits Reflection

Finding your purpose is not as hard as most people think. Believe it or not, you probably already know your purpose. At the S.K.I.R.T.S. in the Boardroom: Set No Limits Summit, we teach that your purpose is what drives you. It is what makes you passionate. It is not some elusive phenomenon that we can never grasp. Because you were created on purpose to live with purpose, you are supposed to know what your purpose entails. The sooner you realize that, the sooner you walk with direction. Remember, step one is to acknowledge the purpose you possess. Step two is to unlock it. And, honey, only you hold the key. You can begin your purpose-driven discovery below, and gather more valuable insights at www.skirtsintheboardroom.com. Enjoy!

PRIORITIES

List your top ten values (for example, career, individual, family, relationship, spiritual, community, economic, health, and recreational values).

1. _____

2. _____

3. _____

4. _____

5. _____

6. _____

7. _____

8. _____

9. _____

10. _____

PRIORITIZE

Now rank your top three values *and* write a sentence about why each is important to you:

1. _____

2. _____

3. _____

Balance is central to direction. Use the space provided in the box below to reflect on how you are spending your time in relation to your stated priorities.

_____

_____

_____

_____

_____

PLEASURES
What are things you like to do?

1. _____
2. _____
3. _____
4. _____
5. _____
6. _____

What are things that you do *not* like to do?

1. _____
2. _____
3. _____
4. _____
5. _____
6. _____

PROFICIENCIES
What things are you *good* at doing?

1. _____
2. _____
3. _____
4. _____
5. _____
6. _____

PASSION

What motivates you?

1. _____

2. _____

3. _____

4. _____

5. _____

6. _____

What is your dream job? What would you do if money were no object?

1. _____

2. _____

What impact would you like to make in the following areas?

Community: _____

Career: _____

Family: _____

Social: _____

Relationships: _____

Creating a Purpose Statement

You have probably heard of corporate mission and vision statements. Companies use these statements as directives to help keep business operations on course. It is also a means of succinctly communicating to the world the company's ultimate purpose.

This is your opportunity to do the same. If you do not already have a purpose statement, let's create one now. If you do have one, let's see if it needs updating. A purpose statement is not complex. It is a simple sentence that combines your proficiencies, your pleasures, and your passions.

SAMPLE FORMAT

Here is a sample format using the information you outlined in the earlier exercises.

My purpose is to fulfill my passion of _____ *(insert passion)*

by demonstrating my _____ *(insert proficiency and/or pleasure)*

in order to _____ *(insert desired impact)*

SAMPLE PURPOSE STATEMENT

My purpose is to fulfill my passion of *motivating others* by demonstrating my *skill of public speaking* in order to *equip others to maximize their potential.*

YOUR PURPOSE STATEMENT

_____

_____

_____

_____

_____

Share your purpose statement with other women at www
.skirtsintheboardroom.com.

Quick Tip

Your purpose is like a dressing room. Use it to assess the things in your life that fit.

Chapter 4

Commitment

No Substitute Is as Sweet as Real Sugar

Com•mit•ment (*n*) the trait of sincere and steadfast fixity of purpose.

The single most important factor in achieving any measure of *sustainable* success is commitment. There is no substitute for commitment, and no shortcut around it. A contract without commitment is just words on a piece of paper. Without commitment, an athlete with all of the potential in the world never becomes a champion. There is no such thing as an uncommitted leader. There is no such thing as an uncommitted achievement. And there can be no such thing as long-lasting success in your career without commitment.

You see, mediocrity and commitment cannot co-exist. It is an all-or-nothing, take-it-or-leave-it deal. You are either committed or you are not. More importantly, commitment is not reflected in *what you say,* it is manifested in *what you do.* It is more than a promise, a pledge, or a vow of assurance. Commitment is simple. Commitment is consistent. Commitment is reliable. Commitment is action.

In fact, commitment is the catalyst for *all* action. If you pledge yourself to a certain goal or specific purpose, then you act in alignment with that pledge by fulfilling your promise—that is, if your commitment is sincere. Commitment distinguishes what we *want* from what we *intend.* I have said before that wanting will never get you anywhere.

We all want to be successful, including your competition. Wanting success is not enough.

To W.A.N.T. is to *Wait and Nothing Transpires.*

I get resume after resume from college students, graduates from business schools, and graduating law-school students who want a job in professional sports and therefore apply with our sports agency. If someone sends me a resume and then never follows up, I assume that they are not all that committed. I could be wrong, but that person has not given me a reason to think otherwise. I will not hire a person who is not committed, so I won't waste my time following up with that person— not when I have others who will consistently check in and express their interest.

Commitment is vital to our agency's success. We have *worked* for every client that we have. I work extra hard as a woman business owner of a sports agency. I have to. So I expect the same hunger, passion, and enthusiasm from anyone looking to join our company. Commitment is the number-one filter that I use in building my team and choosing business partners.

The reason I value commitment so deeply is that it is one of those things that you cannot teach, but which makes all the difference in the world. Confidence can be developed. Communication can be worked on. But a fundamental ethos, or, as I like to say, a commitment to commitment, cannot be taught.

At EDGE 3M, we recruit blue-chip, high-net-worth clients. The professional sports industry is extremely competitive. There are agencies that are much bigger than mine and have been around longer. However, we have been able to compete toe-to-toe with those larger firms because of our commitment to our clients. Bigger isn't always better. Commitment is always better. That becomes a key selling point for my agency when we are recruiting new clients. Our clients do not get lost in the shuffle. They do not get neglected. Our clients can trust that we are acting in their best interest. That level of commitment goes a long way in making any business a success.

At ME Unlimited, I do a lot of seminars for professionals in sales, financial services, and competitive industries on how commitment serves as a value-enhancer in developing business. You will hear the word *no* more times than you will hear the word *yes*. But if you are committed and do the right things, then eventually you will get a "yes."

Additionally, through ME Unlimited, I do a great deal of performance coaching for c-suite level executives on how commitment can transform the culture of the work environment. At the end of the day, commitment is about expectations and intentions. A committed woman expects the best and intends to use her savvy to make things happen.

Talk Is Cheap, Actions Speak

You have probably heard the saying that talk is cheap. Well, the point of this chapter is to emphasize that actions speak. The key is to do the right things the right way in order to advance your career or your business. The problem is that we live in a microwave society where everyone expects immediate results and immediate success. Remember: Anything worth having is worth working for.

The perception today is that nobody wants to earn anything. Everybody wants something for nothing. There is a misguided sense of entitlement that many people have, particularly young adults in the workplace. I have seen and experienced it. And it is a concern that Human Resource professionals share with me all the time. Do not be one of those people. Your commitment to your job, your career, your clients, and your reputation is how you *earn* your success—success that will last and stand the test of time.

So what makes commitment work? I believe that the key to authentic commitment is being committed to something greater than you. Think about that for a moment.

Let me explain. When I was younger, I never wanted to disappoint or embarrass my parents. I valued their opinion. I appreciated their love and support. So I was committed to living my life in a way that demonstrated integrity. I have always been committed to something greater than myself. It helps to keep life in perspective, and to keep my business focused.

In business, *authentic* commitment helps to guide your actions and decisions, which are based on principle, not on becoming more powerful. There is a big difference. Think of someone in a position of leadership that you admire or respect. It could be a current or former boss, a project manager, or a coworker. Now think of someone in a position of leadership whom you do *not* admire or respect. In all likelihood, the difference between the person you admire and the one you don't is probably reflected in that person's commitment to something greater than him- or herself.

For example, let's take the leader you like. You would probably say that that person is committed to excellence, motivating others, or selflessness. As for the leader whom you do not like, you would probably say that that person is committed to advancing his or her own self-interest. That person is probably more concerned with money, power, politics, or his or her own positioning. So much so that you have absolutely no desire to do any more than you have to for this person. You'll do just enough to get by. Whereas, when you work for a leader that you like, one who is committed to a higher cause, you cannot wait to go above and beyond. When you are committed to something greater than yourself, great things happen.

The Six Elements of Commitment: *The Six Ds*

Commitment is a reflection of six factors that I refer to as the Six Ds: Desire, Drive, Determination, Dedication, Diligence, and Discipline. For nearly ten years, I have been speaking to audiences nationwide about these six powerful principles. I have also lived each of these principles. Commitment is what enabled me to land some of the toughest blue-chip clients in the world of professional sports at the tender age of 27. It is also what has enabled me to develop a thriving corporate consulting practice—a seemingly impossible feat for a woman under the age of 30.

While each of the Six Ds of Commitment may seem somewhat similar, they are, as you will see, distinct. Without one ingredient, the formula for success fails. You can have desire, but without drive it's meaningless. You can have desire and drive, but without determination or dedication it's futile. You can even have desire, drive, determination, dedication, and diligence, but if you lack discipline, you stand to lose it all. Let's explore these factors one by one.

DESIRE

Desire is the foundation of commitment, and the starting point of all action. Henry Hazlitt once stated, "A strong passion will ensure success, for the desire of the end will point out the means." You will never fully commit to something that you do not want. Instead, you will simply go through the motions and do just enough to get by. Desire is your aspiration—the root of what you *really* want, and why.

Living a commitment-driven lifestyle requires you to want more out of life and out of your career. When you commit to continually raising the bar by never settling, you desire to do your best and get the best in return. What you want is nowhere near as important as your attitude, willingness, and desire to make it happen. There is a difference between wishing and working, craving and creating, talking and trying, and desiring and doing. But first it is important to understand what it is that you desire in your personal and professional life. When you are able to do what you want, it does not feel like work.

Employers, business owners, and managers should keep this in mind as well. It is important to know what your individual team members want, or at least their motivation for working on a particular project. I have several employees who work on Team EDGE. One of the first questions I ask before someone starts with the agency is about their motivation for working with us. Second, I ask them about their short-term and long-term goals. Third, I ask them what types of projects interest them most.

If I bring that person aboard, I do a few things that help increase that person's desire to work for us with a committed work ethic. First, I explain specifically the reasons why that person was hired. Maybe it was their level of creativity, their personality, or their attention to detail. I explain how that particular characteristic will help EDGE 3M grow and sustain business. The conversation usually goes something like this:

Congratulations! We are excited at the prospect of you joining our agency. I like to set clear expectations up front, so understand that my intentions are two-fold. One, to provide quality service to our clients, which enables us to consistently grow our business. Two, to provide you, as a member of our team, with an opportunity to grow, learn the industry, make valuable contacts, and contribute in a way that maximizes your potential. We want and expect you to demonstrate your strengths and talent.

Of course, not every project is creative. Not every project is glamorous. But every project and every task, whether it is sending a fax or organizing a celebrity VIP list, is equally important to our team's success. We are offering you a position in particular because I believe in you, I believe in your talent, and I believe in your ability to get things done. We have high expectations, but we only hire people who we believe can surpass them. If this sounds like something you want to be a part of, and you're willing to work hard, then welcome aboard.

Notice a few things. I explain my expectations and my goals. I let the person know that my desire is the same as their desire—for that person to grow. People who feel as though they are a part of a team are more motivated. I like to give people responsibility and let them know that I trust them. I don't believe in coddling anyone. I don't have time. I don't give "crappy" projects to anyone. There is no such thing if you frame work assignments the right way. Everything is a part of the larger vision. If someone is assigned to research or developing proposals, it is just one piece of the puzzle. It needs to get done. For that reason, you *must* communicate your vision for a particular project or client to your team members.

People buy into vision. So, I explain the vision for an event before giving an assignment. I explain who the client is and what the client wants to accomplish off the field. If it's a corporate client, I explain their brand objectives. That way everyone working on the project is motivated by a desire to fulfill a vision, not just to complete a miscellaneous task.

When you are able to work on what you want, it comes more easily. When I prepare to go speak to an audience or conduct a seminar, I can usually outline an entire 60- to 90-minute keynote speech in 10 to 15 minutes. It comes easily to me because I'm doing something that I want to do. I have an intense desire to help people live their dreams.

On the other hand, when I used to prepare the sports agency's weekly accounting expenses for bookkeeping, I struggled. I understood *how* to do the bookkeeping. But I hated it. I always put it off until the last minute. I did it because the bookkeeping needed to get done. I believe that every business owner should personally monitor every single penny that goes in and out of the company for the first year.

So I made a commitment to do my own bookkeeping. But I never liked it or wanted to do it. But I had to do it. It always took me longer than it should. I realized that crunching numbers and inputting data is not my thing. Then I hired my accountant. She absolutely loves numbers. I like money, but she loves (and I mean *loves*) numbers! I noticed that bookkeeping came to her easily and effortlessly. She was meticulous and thorough. She was even passionate about making sure I understood what was happening and why. She loved educating her clients about compliance and accounting standards. I realized that I was wasting energy trying to do something that I had no desire to do. My company would run much more efficiently by having people exercise their strengths.

> *A pinch of desire is greater than a pound of talent.*
> —Marshawn Evans

Clearly, sometimes you have to do things that you don't like in any job—especially when you're starting a new career or a new business. Sometime you have to get the coffee, send the fax, and complete the filing. Early in your career, you have to be humble. You'll get assignments that you do not like. As a business owner, I guarantee that you will have to wear multiple hats and do whatever it takes to get the job done. No business starts on day one with a support staff. Sacrifice is a part of life and part of professional growth. It is also the ultimate sign of authentic commitment.

The bigger point I am making is that recognizing what you want will help you to focus your commitments. You cannot do everything. You might as well do what you desire when you have the choice. You won't be able to demonstrate commitment without desire. People will see through you in a heartbeat. I know you can tell when a person really wants something. There is a reason for that. True desire breeds true commitment.

> *Why did I want to win? Because I didn't want to lose!*
> —Max Schmelling

DRIVE

Drive is what motivates you. It is a compelling internal motivating force that propels you to action. Drive is going with the goal (what you desire) in mind. No goal, no go. If you care enough about accomplishing a particular result, than you will certainly do what it takes to attain it. The question is, What motivates you? What drives you to do your best?

Some people are motivated by accolades and recognition. Others are motivated by money. Some are motivated by the desire to please other people. I had a client who once told me that he was driven by a fear of failure. Something drives each of us. Just as a car cannot run without fuel, you cannot run a committed race without drive. The important thing to remember is that nothing should motivate you more than you motivate yourself. Too many external factors will come and go. You must determine for yourself what you will allow to motivate you.

Once EDGE 3M started to grow, our agency started getting more and more requests to do marketing work outside the realm of sports and entertainment. All of the sudden we had projects all over the map. I found myself stressed, working 18-hour days, and I began to lose the excitement and joy I once had for my work.

The problem was that I had become motivated by opportunity. I thought, Hey, there is nothing wrong with opportunity, right? I jumped at every quality opportunity that came my way if the price tag was right. Big mistake. We made a lot of money, but I began to lose my desire for the business. We had too much work. We were spread too thin. At the time, I was not driven to do my best. I was driven to just get the projects done. When that happens, the quality of the work will always suffer.

Opportunity can be misleading. Every door is not your door. You cannot fully commit to everything that comes your way, so you will have to be selective about how you commit your time. Understand (and remember) what drives you (good and bad), and use that to guide your choices in developing your career or your business. Sometimes you have to say "no" or refer a client somewhere else. If you are unfocused, you will eventually become uncommitted. Commit to recognize, restore, replenish, and retain your sense of drive.

DETERMINATION

I like to think of determination as your strength of mind. It represents your willpower and staying power. It is your stamina, your endurance, and your willingness to see something thru to the end. As Mario Andretti once stated, "Desire is the key to motivation, but it's the determination and commitment to an unrelenting pursuit of your goal—a commitment to excellence—that will enable you to attain the success you seek."

I am moved by people who have resolved in their mind that they will reach their goals. I look at someone like Oprah Winfrey. Oprah grew up poor, and endured sexual, physical, and emotional abuse. She was told that she was not attractive enough to be on television. She was told that her nose was too big, her eyes too wide, and her skin too brown. Now, many say that she is the most powerful woman in the world.

Oprah was (and still is) a woman with determination. She resolved firmly in her mind that she would pursue a career in broadcasting. She does what she loves (notice the *desire*), and she is *driven* by a commitment to help other people. As a result, she has been *determined* to overcome obstacles. Her commitment to her vision has paid off. One reason Oprah has become successful in television is because her commitment to people and inspiring excellence is sincere. Authentic commitment naturally creates success. You cannot copy it. You cannot imitate it. You can only be sincerely determined when your desire and drive are equally sincere.

When I practiced law with a large law firm, I showed up every morning ready to give my best. However, I was not passionate about the work. I was not helping people, which is a part of my calling. No matter how much I set my mind to doing a good job, the effort never came naturally. I had to pull long hours, but there was no motivation to work extra hard or extra long. I spent a period of time away from my law firm to do a fellowship with a legal-aid nonprofit organization.

The purpose of the organization was to provide free legal services to the poor. Every morning I loved getting up to go into the office. I didn't mind staying late and working overtime. It didn't matter that the offices weren't as fancy as the ones at the big law firm. What mattered is that I was able to help my clients get their food stamps so they could feed their families. What mattered is that I was able to help my clients get their unemployment checks following a wrongful termination, or to fight a wrongful eviction filed by a slumlord. I was determined to make sure that my clients' interests were zealously represented. It was then that I realized that practicing law was not the problem. I love the law. I just needed to be motivated by my work. Desire mixed with drive creates dedication. When you are determined, your commitment to your work will show.

> *There are two kinds of people, those who do the work and those who take the credit. Try to be in the first group; there is less competition there.*
> —Indira Gandhi

DEDICATION

Dedication is your devotion to a stated cause, task, or purpose. Dedication also tests your commitment. It is easy to say one thing when times are good, but harder to back that up with action when times are tough. Dr. Robert Schuller once said, "Tough times never last, but tough people do." Uncommitted people don't stick around for too long, but dedicated people stand the test of time.

Many people say that we no longer live in a dedicated society. People will always choose the cheaper, quicker, and faster alternative. While that is partially true, I largely disagree. I believe that people want to be loyal. Employees want to be loyal to their employer. Customers want to be loyal to a service provider. However, they want to receive loyalty first in order to give it in return. This principle became clear to me when I started working with one of my first NFL clients. I had spent about eight months trying to get this player as a client. I consistently called with media opportunities.

I was *beyond* prepared for meetings. I put together PowerPoint displays and color presentations about what the company had in mind for enhancing his brand and increasing his exposure. However, month after month went by, and there was no commitment. About seven and a half months into the recruiting process, I called the player with another media opportunity. I had been calling periodically for the past month with no answer, so this time I was just thankful that he answered the phone! It turned out that the player was unable to do the radio interview; however, he asked me if my company would plan his celebrity weekend. I said "Of course!" That event became one of the defining events for our agency.

Over 45 NFL and NBA players from around the country came to town for the celebrity weekend. Not only was it a good time for us to impress our client, it was also an opportunity for us to showcase our work to all of the other players who were attending the series of events. It enabled us to gain valuable corporate sponsorship relationships and elevated our profile in the industry. That would not have happened if I wasn't dedicated on several levels.

I had to be dedicated to this client. He needed to see persistence to believe that we were the real deal. Furthermore, we had to be dedicated to doing a stellar job once we got the work. He was extremely impressed with our work, and he committed to becoming an exclusive client—meaning that we would have the exclusive rights to market him and secure his endorsements. Athletes can be extremely loyal—sometimes to the wrong people. But usually they are looking for someone they can trust—someone who is dedicated to working with them in the good times and the bad times. If you show dedication, your clients will respond in the same way.

DILIGENCE

Diligence is a reflection of your commitment. It manifests in your attentiveness, thoroughness, awareness, and attention to detail. A diligent person is someone who pays attention to the things that others ignore. I truly believe that the difference is in the details. If you want to impress your boss or your clients, then think ahead. Raise issues that no one else is taking into consideration. Spot problems before they appear. Take notice when something is not right, and offer a solution or a suggestion for how to rectify the situation.

I once hired a young lady to work with my company on a provisional basis. I initially stated that we would hire her on a month-to-month basis, and that the first month would be a trial period. Well, she really impressed me (and that is *very* difficult to do). I was impressed with her persistence, which was why I hired her in the first place. I became equally impressed with her attention to detail.

She would point out things that I had missed and she would ask questions when something did not match up. She increased her value by being concerned about the work at hand, not just about doing the work. I began to trust her because she demonstrated a commitment to make sure the work was done right, not just done. Being diligent will separate you from the pack. Most people do just enough to get by. If you go above and beyond by being aware, detail-oriented, and meticulous, your work will not go unnoticed. You will get increased responsibility, increased trust, and increased opportunity for advancement in your career.

DISCIPLINE

Discipline is about having restraint. As I've alluded to throughout the book, success if not about doing everything you *can* do, it is about doing everything you *should* do. That implies, naturally, that there are certain things (and people) you should avoid. I have to be very disciplined in how I use my time.

Every day I get dozens of e-mails from people who want to schedule a meeting over breakfast, lunch, or dinner. Most of my days are filled with work and client representation. If it's not sports, marketing, or negotiation, then I'm on the road at a speaking engagement. That doesn't leave much time for in-person meetings. So I have had to become quite disciplined with how I spend my time. I also need time for myself. So do you! You cannot give all of your time to people, places, and things—you will have nothing left for yourself.

At the S.K.I.R.T.S. in the Boardroom: Set No Limits Summit, we teach women how to make choices that will lead to optimal career advancement and growth. Remember, free will is something that the Creator left to each of us. Choices are the most powerful thing you possess. Do not give up your personal power by allowing others to dictate and control how you spend your time. You wouldn't let someone else spend your money—don't let someone else spend your time.

Being disciplined is fundamental to being committed. Being disciplined means you have a filter. It means that you can show restraint when necessary with regard to what you do, and what you say. There have been times that I've wanted to speak up against something that I disagreed with, but I held my tongue because the timing was not right. I was committed to a larger goal and objective, and speaking up would not have been productive—not at that particular time.

Discipline is about choices. You show your commitment based on the choices you make. Studying is a choice. Training is a choice. Personal development is a choice. Working hard and putting your best foot forward is also a choice. Disciple is the conscious decision to be and do your best by exercising self-control, focus, and structure. To succeed in and even get to the boardroom, girlfriend, you must be committed to a life of commitment.

The Seven Commitment Commandments for Women

1. Thou Shalt Pay Attention to Detail
2. Thou Shalt Anticipate Obstacles before They Occur
3. Thou Shalt Avoid Overcommitment
4. Thou Shalt Be on Time
5. Thou Shalt Be Optimistic
6. Thou Shalt Follow up
7. Thou Shalt Follow Through

Tangible Benefits of Commitment

There are several benefits of making a commitment to authentic commitment in your career. For women, there are five in particular: (1) Buy-In, (2) Loyalty, (3) Expanded Opportunity, (4) Excitement, and (5) Reputation.

BENEFIT ONE: *BUY–IN*

Commitment creates BUY-IN. When you invest yourself in a project, your boss and your clients will invest in you and believe in you. It is about more than just investing your time. It's about TLC.

When you demonstrate that you care about outcomes and achieving results, others will become more open to your ideas and suggestions. They will also buy-in to the idea (even subconsciously) of helping you to advance your career goals and objectives. That produces a win-win situation for everyone.

BENEFIT TWO: *LOYALTY*

Commitment creates LOYALTY. When you've committed to your clients by going the extra mile, showing your competence, and doing a good job, your clients become more loyal to you. They almost have no choice. If there is only one store in town that carries a special type of lightbulb, then you have to go to that store. If there is more than one choice of store location, then you'll probably go to the store that is most convenient and provides the best service.

The same is true in business. If you can (1) produce a quality product or service, and then (2) make your product or service consistently convenient to the customer, then you're in business! My clients come to us because our agency is a one-stop shop for everything related to branding. That's convenient.

If we can couple convenience with quality service, then we have a customer for life. By handling every aspect of a client's branding, we also make ourselves indispensable. That is, we increase our value in multiple areas such that it makes it easier (and sometimes cheaper) to stay with us than to hire multiple companies.

BENEFIT THREE: *EXPANDED OPPORTUNITY*

Commitment creates *expanded opportunity*. When I was practicing law in the traditional sense, I would usually get a very small piece of a case—typically research, which I always found quite boring. However, if I did a good job on the research, then I would usually get more responsibility. Eventually, I would be handling most of the case altogether. Because I knew the research and I worked with the clients, I knew all of the details.

The lead partner on the case needed me because I was the access point for all of the key information. If, on top of being an organized and efficient gatekeeper, I also performed well, then I just expanded the likelihood of getting additional responsibility on the current case and on ones in the future. The same holds true with my employees and my contractors. All of my contractors know that they are auditioning for work every time we call with a new project. If they do a good job on one project, they'll likely get the next one (loyalty). We will also be more comfortable in referring that contractor to others for more work. And I'll likely look at increasing the scope of work given to that contractor internally, as well.

I have a client who fired his sports agent because his agent was lazy. He did just enough to get by. The client (my client) didn't feel as though his agent was fully committed. Instead of gaining expanded opportunity, the agent lost all of the client's business. The client went on to sign a major contract a year later. The agent missed out on that commission . . . a huge commission. Expanded opportunity will always come because of a commitment to excellence on the small things. Do not despise small beginnings.

BENEFIT FOUR: *EXCITEMENT*

Commitment creates EXCITEMENT. When you're committed, you generate a contagious energy that infects others with excitement. That happens because people respond to passion. If you're passionate about your work, others will be passionate about supporting you. Your passion will translate into increased opportunity, increased loyalty, and increased pay. I like giving bonuses to team members who demonstrate their passion. If someone is doing just enough to get by, then I have no motivation to reward them for mediocrity—beyond paying what is owed. Passion will make others excited about rewarding you.

The same thing happens when you find committed and passionate clients. I can honestly say that I enjoy every one of my agency's clients. They are fun to work with, but they are not all equally consistent in terms of being responsive. Some clients get back to you right away, and others drag their feet. When we work with a client who is timely and excited about a particular project, then that increases the passion and excitement for our entire team. Passion ignites passion.

BENEFIT FIVE: *REPUTATION*

Commitment creates your REPUTATION. If your work ethic reflects a commitment to excellence, meaning that you are reliable, consistent, and you do great work, then you build a solid reputation. There is no substitute for reputation. You cannot buy it, you can only build it. Advertising without a good reputation is wasted money. A good team without a good reputation is wasted talent. And a good product or service without a good reputation is a wasted idea. You need a good reputation.

For those just starting out in business, you might think you're handicapped by the lack of work history. Not true. You have a clean slate with no negative history. That's a good thing. The same holds true for those of you in the workplace. You can build your reputation brick-by-brick simply by being consistent, reliable, and trustworthy. Character and integrity are extremely important, yet hard to find. That alone will distinguish you in the marketplace. Follow up when you get a business card. Call people back. Be professional. Send thank-you cards. Do your research so that you can be competent in your industry and know your customers. Most people neglect the small things, not realizing that those things add up to make a big difference.

My business has grown largely (and quickly) by referrals. Being referred is less expensive and more effective than traditional business development and recruiting. There is a *big* lesson here for any business owner, employer, manager, or anyone in sales or human resources.

What other people say about you is more important than what you say about yourself. That's why references are so important.

When I was a law student, the two job offers I received after my first year of law school came via an initial referral from another lawyer. Those law firms receive hundreds of resumes. My first few clients in the sports agency came through a referral. That has led to even more clients coming via referrals. Do you have any idea how much money that saves me in airfare, hotel, ground transportation, and meals, alone? I save more money by doing a good job.

If an existing client refers a potential client to me, then I'm twice as likely to get that person or company as a client under contract. On the other hand, if I make a cold call to a potential client who knows nothing about the agency, then the process is much longer, and with a lower success rate. I have to build goodwill from scratch in the latter scenario. Time is money. So, it costs more in the long run. Take your time to do a great job for your clients or your boss. Be cautious of growing too fast without the capacity to execute on your commitments. Talent means nothing without the ability to execute. By committing wisely, you build a reputation to last a lifetime.

> *Whoever said anybody has a right to give up?*
> —Marian Wright Edelman

Lessons for M.E. (Motivation and Empowerment)

Anything worth having is worth working for. Commitment is how you earn your career success. Quick success usually leads to quicker loss. Why? There is no solid foundation. Success is built upon a foundation of patience interlocked with perseverance. Timing is everything. As the saying goes, slow and steady wins the race.

The emphasis is on steady. Many get stuck on the slow. Sluggishly waiting for opportunity is like waiting for Mr. Right. He may or may not show up. When it comes to your date with success, it is okay for YOU to make the first move! Remember, the single most important factor in achieving any measure of *sustainable* success is commitment.

The six manifestations of a committed woman, or the Six Ds, include Desire, Drive, Determination, Dedication, Diligence, and Discipline. Your commitment results in five distinct benefits that build business and enhance careers. Those benefits include (1) Buy-In, (2) Loyalty, (3) Expanded Opportunity, (4) Excitement, and (5) Reputation. For women, there is no substitute for commitment, and no shortcut around it.

Set No Limits Reflection

You cannot make it in business and get into the boardroom without commitment. You can learn more tips on establishing a career trademarked by commitment at www.skirtsintheboardroom.com. Let's assess now how you can develop it. The questions below are designed to enhance your career as you establish a committed style of day-to-day operation.

A Committed Value System

How do I want my customers, colleagues, and superiors to describe me? List three descriptions.

1. _____

2. _____

3. _____

What five character traits demonstrate commitment in my career field?

1. _____

2. _____

3. _____

4. _____

5. _____

Which of the above areas need development in my professional life? List five items that you wish to improve.

1. _____

2. _____

3. _____

4. _____

5. _____

COMMITMENT ASSESSMENT

What do I DESIRE for my ideal job and career?

Job: _____

Career: _____

What DRIVES me in my job and career?

Job: _____

Career: _____

What actions demonstrate my DETERMINATION in my job and my career?

Job: _____

Career: _____

What actions demonstrate my DEDICATION to my job and my career?

Job: _____

Career: _____

What behaviors and values demonstrate my level of DILIGENCE in my job and career?

Job: _____

Career: _____

What areas are in need of more DISCIPLINE in my job and career?

Job: _____

Career: _____

COMMITMENT ACTION PLAN

Development Commitment: What new behavior or skill will I commit to developing in order to help me reach my commitment goals?

_____

_____

_____

Progress Indicators: How will I know that I have created new behaviors or skills?

_____

_____

_____

Resources: What resources will help me develop these skills and behaviors?

_____

_____

_____

Part Two

Serving Up Some Homemade Style and Substance

Part Two focuses on transformation. The four critical areas outlined in these chapters are the qualities that highly successful women consistently demonstrate: communication (how you listen is as important as what you say), connections (networking), creativity (resourcefulness and what you can create out of thin air), and captivation (creating your personal brand).

Chapter 5

Communication

If You've Got It, Flaunt It

**Com•mu•ni•ca•tion (*n*) the art and technique of
effectively imparting information or ideas.**

Women who advance in their careers, along with women who have
successful companies, are women with superior speaking skills. Plain
and simple: Success in business is not about good ideas. It is about being
able to *sell* good ideas.

Ideas, like opinions, are a dime a dozen. Almost everyone, it seems,
has a great idea. What separates a great idea from an actual reality is the
person who has a great idea *and* the ability to sell that idea. It's kind of
like me right now. For the past year I've been writing this book. In
passing, when people ask me what I'm working on or just make polite
conversation and I mention that "I'm writing a book," almost everyone I
run into says, "I have a great idea for a book!"

Not "What's your book about?" or "Who is it for?" or even "Would I
like it?," but straight to "I have a great idea for a book!" Oftentimes, when
the person (inevitably) shares their great idea, it *is* actually pretty good. I
encourage them by saying, "You should write that down." I've even
pointed them to my web site, where they can find my e-mail address and
other contact information, and told them to "keep me informed" about
their progress.

And many of them walk away, I'm sure, determined to do just that. But I know that the minute they hit a snag, or get blocked, or life gets in the way, or the car breaks down, or the printer runs out of ink, they're going to lose their inspiration and give up.

Out of all those people, in airports and hotel ballrooms and conference and community centers and libraries and coffee shops, out of all those business cards and URLs I've given out, nobody's ever called to update me on their great idea for a book. I can't blame them, but I wish I could share with them the gift of communication so that they could share their great idea with the world.

Next to confidence, the second most important factor determining the bounds of your success is your ability to communicate. Being able to effectively communicate your ideas and relate to people will determine how much success—along with how much money—you stand to make in your lifetime. For women looking to make it big in business or to hold their ground in the boardroom, impeccable communication skills are vital, not optional.

Of all of the things that women are self-conscious about, however, their communication skills usually rank toward the top of the list. There is good reason. First, we have been fed a bunch of bull! For ages, we have been stereotyped as ineffective communicators. Men tell us that we talk too much. Some tell us that we don't talk enough, while others tell us that we never really have anything meaningful to say at all (like they do?). In a society in which the male style of communication and leadership has become the standard, it can be challenging for us to find our own, unique voices.

Second, we believed the bull. When I started my first company, Communication Counts! eight years ago, I spent much of my time coaching individuals, athletes, entertainers, personalities, politicians, and beauty queens on the keys to effective communication. The majority of my clients were women. I was initially surprised by the need for motivation as a critical element of the coaching. I really had to spend time with clients to help them see that this was an area in which they could succeed. Many, maybe even most, felt that they were inadequate communicators. They fundamentally saw themselves as incapable.

To this day, I see the same thing with athletes and professionals—male and female. So this isn't something solely endemic to women. However, I think we struggle with the psychological aspect of communication more than do men. Men are expected to be good communicators, while we are not. Plus, as you'll see later in this chapter, there are gender differences in communication.

Remember, however, that *perception of self always influences performance*. Very rarely will you be able to do something well if you cannot first envision yourself in that action as a successful reality. Much of success is mental. It is about getting over fear, and functioning in your gifts. Only after you accept and embrace that you are capable (yes, you!) of communicating well can you hone your skills.

You'll never get where you want to go if you can't explain how you plan to get there. You'll never get what you want, if you do not know how to ask for it. And, you'll never maximize your potential if you fail to see yourself as capable. Winning starts in the mind. In other words, you can do this. You can do this well. In fact, speaking with excellence is in your DNA.

Talking versus Connecting: *Convert to PDF!*

There are those who believe that communicating is simple. I disagree. *Talking* is easy. *Connecting* with people is always more challenging—especially for women. In order to connect, you must first understand the tools you've been given to craft your message. At ME Unlimited, we teach that "connective communication" is a product of three key interrelated elements (PDF).

1. Preparation
2. Delivery
3. Flexibility

PREPARATION

The first key to communicating well is to be *prepared*. You need to know your audience, know your objectives, and then work your message backward. The same holds true for both one-on-one briefings and large-scale presentations. Knowing your audience will help you set your objectives. Knowing your objectives will help you organize your message.

The following exhibit shows how your preparation plan might look in 3-D.

$$1 \qquad\qquad 2 \qquad\qquad 3$$

PREPARATION PLAN = AUDIENCE → OBJECTIVES → MESSAGE

Knowing your audience requires a bit of selflessness. You must be more attuned to the M.I.N.D. (*M*otivations, *I*nterests, *N*eeds, and *D*esires) of your listener (i.e., your boss, your colleague, or your client) than your own. Everybody has a motivation. Why should this person be motivated to listen to you? That's your first question. To explain, let me walk you through a hypothetical business development scenario regarding a client pitch in which I'm keeping the client in M.I.N.D..

- ◆ *The task:* Secure a WNBA athlete as a client (that's women's pro basketball).
- ◆ *The challenge:* We have no WNBA clients.
- ◆ *The audience:* Ima Hooper, a current WNBA player and potential client.

I'm scheduled to meet with Ima Hooper over coffee to talk to her about our agency. The first thing I do is research her background, study her profile, learn her stats, her education, family history, everything I can find. While doing my research, I learn that Ima is interested in philanthropy, particularly in improving self-esteem in young girls. So I now know a few things.

First, Ima is interested in her marketing and branding, or else she would not have agreed to a meeting. I can tell from my research that she does not have very many endorsements. (That will be a key selling point.) Second, I know that Ima is interested in philanthropy. So, I can do some more research on possible youth programs that we can link her with as spokesperson or advocate. (I'll stop there—I could go on and on with the amount of detail we go into when developing a branding plan.)

Now that I know a bit more about Ima, I can set my preliminary objectives for the meeting (some of those might change as the meeting takes place, but I'll touch on adapting in just a moment). My primary communication objectives are two-fold.

1. Introduce Ima to our agency.
2. Explain how our service offering can help elevate Ima's profile.

I can now detail and organize my message around those two primary objectives. To prepare, you need to know your audience, determine your objectives, and then plan your message accordingly. You want to tailor your message to your audience by focusing on their M.I.N.D. (remember: Motivations, Interests, Needs, and Desires).

DELIVERY

Here is the big enchilada! Performance (your execution and actual delivery) is what most people focus on and think about when it comes to communication. As complex as it may seem, I am going to break down the aspects of performance into three primary dynamics of delivery.

1. Verbal Dynamics (word choice)
2. Vocal Dynamics (sound)
3. Visual Dynamics (demeanor)

If I were to ask you the most important factor in communicating—the factor that makes the greatest impression on your listener—which of the performance dynamics would you guess reigns supreme: verbal, vocal, or visual? Better yet, in the following list, express your answer using percentages. What percent of the message retained by your listener is influenced by each type of dynamic?

Verbal Dynamics   (Word Choice)   _____%

Vocal Dynamics   (Sound)   _____%

Visual Dynamics   (Demeanor)   _____%

Many people guess that word choice is most important. I see women (and men) stress endlessly over trying to pick the right words, instead of focusing on getting the entire message across. Words are only one part of a message. In fact, the breakdown is as follows.

Verbal Dynamics	(Word Choice)	<u>7 %</u>
Vocal Dynamics	(Sound)	<u>38 %</u>
Visual Dynamics	(Demeanor)	<u>55 %</u>

That means that most of what we say is not actually retained! Our listeners will be impacted more by our demeanor and how we sound—and that's affected by our level of confidence. I know, it's hard when new information goes against the grain of all we've been told, but this is the reality and to succeed we must heed it and respect it. Don't skimp on word choice, by any means, but to that end don't disregard the impression you make when you speak and even how you sound.

We spend time worrying about words that won't be remembered. Now, don't get me wrong. Your word choice is important. It contributes to your credibility, which is necessary to keep anyone's attention. Your listeners, especially men, automatically tune out anyone who comes across as unbelievable, incapable, incompetent, or untrustworthy.

So your word choice, the substance of your message, is critical. However, you need to understand that *most* of what you say will not be remembered. That's why you take notes when you go to a meeting. Our minds can only retain so much. But impressions go much deeper than mere words. How you deliver the words is just as important as the words you choose.

People may not remember everything you say, but they will always remember how you made them feel. That's the difference between connecting and talking.

FLEXIBILITY

Women have to be able to adjust. It is important to expand your communicative repertoire and then adapt your style to fit various situations as they arise. This is what power communicators are able to do. You cannot have a one-size-fits-all mentality when it comes to communication. You have to listen. You have to process. And you have to adjust your message and your delivery accordingly.

> *Listening, not imitation, may be the*
> *sincerest form of flattery.*
> —Dr. Joyce Brothers

Listening requires three assessment steps—the 3 Rs.

1. First, you have to *RECEIVE* what your listener is telling you. The message given by the other person may be different than what you originally had in mind, and might cause your original objectives to change.
2. Next, you should *REFLECT* upon what was said, how it was said, and why it was said. Focus on the person's M.I.N.D.. Why someone says something is always more important than what they say.
3. Finally, *RESPOND* to the why. I recommend paraphrasing what you think you just heard to make sure you are on the same page, and that you truly understand your listener's perspective. Now, as you adjust your message, you are responding based on what you have received and reflected upon.

In the hypothetical scenario with WNBA player Ima Hooper, she might say she is not interested in marketing. I usually don't believe that to be true for a professional athlete, so I need to understand where that sentiment is coming from. I will have to ask about her personal objectives and goals.

In the discussion, I might find that Ima really *is* interested in marketing, but may not understand her marketability and growth potential. Now that I understand why she feels that way, I will need to take a different approach by focusing on what I now know to be her M.I.N.D. She could care less if my motivation is to simply get her as a client. My motivation is to help her reach her goals and live her dreams off the court. It looks like I will have to help her see her marketability before I can discuss a long-term marketing plan.

Remember the 3 Rs: Receive, Reflect, and Respond. In short, connecting, as opposed to talking, will require preparation, performance, and flexibility. Let's continue to delve deeper to see how communication can make you more of an asset at work.

Strategic Information Sharing

As you prepare and deliver your message, keep in mind that your goal is always to communicate in a focused, yet personable manner. By focused, I mean *strategic information sharing*. You want to take into account the listener's M.I.N.D. while still relaying your objectives to get the outcome you desire. Figure 5.1 shows what strategic information sharing looks like.

Strategic information sharing is a key communication tool. If my desired outcome is to land a client, then my message objectives will center on key points that will build trust and confidence in the potential client to hire our agency.

As I mentioned previously, I will need to tailor each of those message points to answer the M.I.N.D. elements of my listener. When you merge

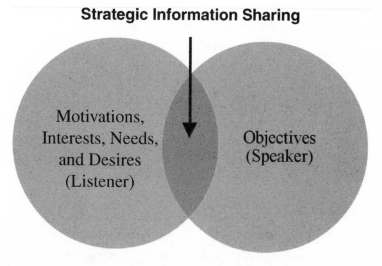

Strategic Information Sharing

Motivations, Interests, Needs, and Desires (Listener)

Objectives (Speaker)

FIGURE 5.1 Strategic Information Sharing

those two elements together, you are strategically sharing information. For some, this may seem too calculated. But most successful outcomes are the result of proper planning. Any commercial you see on television or billboard advertisement takes this principle into account.

A company will spend thousands of dollars researching your M.I.N.D. in order to craft the perfect commercial or advertisement. The desired outcome, of course, is increased sales. There is a reason why companies keep their commercials and advertisements short and simple. They want you to focus on one thing—usually a product, service, or experience. Everything is designed to help you understand the benefits of that product, service or experience.

Focused energy yields more focused results. Practice focusing your communication in the same way. You'll find that you gain (and keep) the attention of your listeners because you are communicating directly to his or her needs. Furthermore, you will achieve better, more focused results. In fact, we have intensive sessions focused on techniques for powerful and assertive communication at the S.K.I.R.T.S. in the Boardroom: Set No Limits Summit. Furthermore, I've provided a wealth of communication tools and resources for you to explore at www.skirt sintheboardroom.com.

Gender Differences in Communication

Men and women are different. When it comes to communication we can be as different as night and day. Although I recognize that each of us is far too unique for me to generalize our behavior, I still want to point out some key differences between men and women in communication styles. These are norms based on research that shows some of the characteristics men and women exhibit.

Understanding the common tendencies for women (and men) will help you to assess and adjust your personal communication style. Knowledge is power! The following sections are about the top five differences between men and women—results versus relationships, particulars versus people, competition versus cooperation, initiation versus interaction; and signals, signals, signals—along with some strategies for becoming a stronger, savvier communicator.

GENDER DIFFERENCE ONE: *RESULTS VERSUS RELATIONSHIPS*

Women tend to be more relationship-oriented and therefore seek to get things by building a relationship first. Have you ever noticed that women seek to get to know a person before focusing on the task at hand?

Conversely, men tend to be more results-oriented, meaning they will likely focus more on the task instead of the people involved. As such, men talk to *give* information, whereas women talk to *gain* information.

In my opinion, there is an inherent advantage in the women's style of communication here. Because we tend to collect information, we have more information in our arsenal. However, asking too many questions can make you seem unsure and reduce the level of confidence that people have in your leadership abilities.

S.K.I.R.T.S. Strategy One: Streamline Your Communication. Focus on information relevant to the task at hand. There is nothing wrong with relationship building. That can be a very strong asset. However, be careful not to waste time with idle chatter that can make you look unfocused, unprepared, or uncertain. People have very short attention spans—especially men! (I'm sure I didn't have to tell you that one.) So, keep pleasantries to a minimum.

While I usually start a meeting or conversation with small talk and maybe a bit of humor, I never want someone else to be forced to point the conversation in the right direction because I'm off on a tangent. Pay attention to the amount of time spent on nonbusiness matters. Time is money. Time is something that you cannot get back. If you waste time, people are less likely to value and respect your opinion and viewpoint. Be pleasant, but be focused!

The best way to gain respect is by competence, so know what you're talking about, too. You can still build relationships by the way in which you interact with others, by respecting other viewpoints, and with your demeanor. Being focused doesn't mean that you check your personality at the door.

GENDER DIFFERENCE TWO: *PARTICULARS VERSUS PEOPLE*

Because women tend to build relationships and good rapport when communicating, they also tend to focus more on people and feelings. On the other hand, men tend to focus on the particulars and facts. As a result, men process information based on logic and reason. While a *big* part of me wants to disagree with that last statement, it is actually true. Men see things in black or white, while women see more gray areas.

One of the quintessential skills I learned as a lawyer is to process information by fact and reason, not opinion. Your opinion means nothing if it is not supported by law or precedent. Ladies, this is how men think, too. They want and need to understand why you feel the way that you do.

S.K.I.R.T.S. Strategy Two: Focus on the WHY, Not the WHAT.   What you think is not as important as why you believe that to be true. The more you can support your opinions with research, fact, and precedent, the more credible and competent you will appear. This is useful to keep in mind whenever you are seeking to change an opinion, or to get someone to see an alternative point of view. This is the key to landing a new client, keeping your existing business, or expanding a service offering. If you can appeal to a person's logic, then you stand a better chance of helping them to see and appreciate your viewpoint.

Most people just state their viewpoint and magically expect others to agree. You might ask, what makes them so special that their opinion is more important (or more right) than yours or mine? See how silly that sounds? This is why you should *not* focus on opinions.

People need for their opinions to be validated in order to feel important, which can be an ego-driven, never-ending battle. This is not a battle you want to fight in the workplace. It is a waste of time and energy. Focus on reason and rationale. By doing so, you remove from the equation the need for personal validation of opinions, which can lead to less productive conversations.

If you can monetize your opinion, that always helps, too. For example, saying that upgrading to a particular (and expensive) software package will save the company $100,000 over the course of a year in increased productivity is far more powerful than saying you prefer this software package because it is the newest on the market. The former statement appeals to the bottom-line profitability interests of the company, whereas the later is just an opinion and personal preference.

When you talk, focus on the particulars, and give people a reason to support you.

That said, there is a time and place where focusing on feeling is important as well. When I meet with a corporation about sponsoring an athlete or celebrity charity event, I'm usually mixing fact *and* feeling. I'll talk about the consumer demographics, the number of brand impressions, and the return on investment. At the same time, I talk about the client's character, personality, and commitment to the community.

If a company feels more connected to a celebrity's charitable interest, they are more likely to partner with that person than if the company simply hears a bunch of facts and figures. So, again, mixing both particulars and people will make you more effective. The key is choosing the appropriate time and place for each approach. In order to make that assessment, I recommend (again) focusing on the M.I.N.D. of your listener. It will always guide you and help you filter (or sometimes fill out) your conversation.

GENDER DIFFERENCE THREE: *COMPETITION VERSUS COOPERATION*

We know that women, generally speaking, tend to build relationships when communicating. As a result we also tend to be more cooperative in our approach, whereas men are more competitive. Men tend to base success on outcomes, not outreach. Men naturally compete to demonstrate their presence, competence, and value.

For example, when I was a young girl, I remember that my brothers and cousins would always race each other. The fastest fella became the leader of the pack. The one who regularly won the video games was the smartest. The one who was the best athlete was the coolest. Men compete to show their value. This is also how they choose their team. They prove themselves. Women, on the other hand, focus on cooperation and making sure that everyone feels included, not excluded.

By *cooperative*, I also mean that women try to find solutions by seeking consensus and avoiding conflict. Conflict, however, can be good and is often necessary. The problem is that women tend to see disagreement as something that destroys relationships. Therefore, we unconsciously tend to look for agreement, which consequently may not be the *best* solution.

S.K.I.R.T.S. Strategy Three: Welcome Disagreement. Don't be afraid of a good fight! Just make sure you fight fair by giving people a chance to express their views. I believe that if everyone is thinking alike, then someone is not thinking. The best ideas are put through the fire, evaluated, and dissected. I believe that a good idea, suggestion, or opinion should *earn* the right to rule the day. I learned this to be especially true when I was on the fourth season of NBC's *The Apprentice* with Donald Trump.

When Mr. Trump gave us a task, our group would assemble to discuss the best strategy. Every time we went with the first idea proposed by someone in the group, we lost—every time! Then, when we ended up as the losing team in the boardroom, where someone was about to be fired, all of the sudden people spoke up and criticized the choices that were made. Where were all of these brilliant suggestions before the task started? No one objected in the beginning because they did not want to be perceived as being difficult.

My philosophy is that the best ideas should earn the right to rule. That means disagreement is inevitable—that is, if everyone is thinking independently with the goal of producing the best outcome. Getting the best result is never easy. I appreciate it when one of my staff disagrees with something that I suggest. It lets me know that they are thinking.

In my world, I want people to contribute—even if it forces me to defend my views. I'm not always right, and I don't always think of everything. In fact, having to think of everything by yourself is draining and leads to more error in the long run. I hire minds, not bodies. There is a big difference!

I get extremely agitated with apathy. I don't like it when someone agrees with everything that I say, or rarely offers an independent opinion. It is one of my biggest pet peeves. To me, it says that you do not care, or that you haven't really thought about something long enough to give an opinion. Again, to me, that indicates that you do not care.

My clients—every single one of them—hire me to have an opinion. And I expect the same thing. I remember when I hired an interior designer for my office. I asked her for her opinion about how we should arrange the clocks on the wall. She said it did not matter. Hmmm. When I asked what color we should use for an accent wall, she said I could go in a few different directions and that anything I chose would be fine. Uh . . . no! That is why I am paying you—for your opinions, for your mind. I realized that she was hesitant to disagree with me because she preferred to avoid conflict. I gain more respect for someone who can speak their mind—especially when I ask. My clients value my opinion, not because I always agree, but because I always have their best interest at heart.

Whatever it is, have an opinion. Do not be afraid to disagree. Do not be afraid to defend your viewpoint. And, do not be so quick to back down or shy away from going against the grain. In the long run, people will respect you.

GENDER DIFFERENCE FOUR: *INITIATION VERSUS INTERACTION*

Men are more likely to initiate conversation, whereas women wait to interact during conversation. As initiators, men are perceived as conversational leaders and women as the followers. I notice that in a meeting or group setting where everyone is quiet, men are usually more likely to speak up and start the conversation. As a result, they immediately establish their presence and dominance and set the tone for the rest of the conversation. Perception is everything.

If someone is perceived as the authority in the room, then that person's views automatically become more valued. When that person talks, others listen. By being an initiator, you garner credibility (as long as you really *do* know what you are talking about). Initiators are able to gain buy-in because they have established credibility through confidence. It can be magnetic and, to some people, it can be intimidating. For women, initiating conversation is one of the most effective tools we can use to be taken seriously in business.

Moreover, men (not women) are also more likely to interrupt people during a conversation. They tend to be less patient. Men will listen to solve a problem or to get what they want accomplished, while not really taking feelings into account. Women, while less likely to interrupt, are far more likely to be interrupted! We often allow someone to cut us off in the middle of a thought. Girl, finish what you are saying! Again, women look for agreement and for ways to soften a message. As a result, we come across as less assertive, and more passive.

S.K.I.R.T.S. Strategy Four: Be the First to Speak Up.   By being the first to speak up, you immediately accomplish several things. First, you demonstrate your confidence and level of self-assuredness. Because women are normally perceived as shy, meek, and less competent, the willingness to confidently speak up and begin a conversation instantly changes the stereotypical perception that we wait for direction. Second, you establish your presence in the conversation and add to your credibility. If people don't express themselves, they are perceived as being less competent and having less to share. You will raise expectations simply by showing you've come to the meeting prepared and ready to contribute and even lead.

Now, as women, we also tend to be more shy in expressing our credentials. You are going to have to get over that very quickly—that is, if you want to excel. You don't have to boast about your accomplishments, but you should not be shy about letting others know that you are qualified in reasoning, request, and representation.

In the spirit of speaking up, you should also take the initiative to ask questions. By asking relevant and timely questions (not simply for the sake of asking questions), you continue to add validity to your viewpoints and experience. In effect, you are demonstrating your value to the project at hand. Why? You are using your mind. You demonstrate that you care about the end result by thinking through possible scenarios and trying to fill in any overlooked holes. Do not just interact during a conversation; take the initiative to get things started!

Gender Difference Five: *Signals, Signals, Signals*

Since the beginning of time, men and women have accused each other of sending mixed signals—meaning we say or do one thing, but really mean another. While both sexes are certainly guilty of this cardinal communication sin, I'm not the slightest bit concerned with the men today!

I'm interested in making sure that *you* are aware of and in control of your body language so that it matches your intended message. We women always want everything to match, right? Making sure that what we say and what we do matches who we are is critically important.

A first impression is a lasting impression. In many situations, it is the *only* impression. Usually, you have just a few moments to communicate who you are, your intelligence, and your capability. You do all of that without ever saying a word. When you do speak, you really reinforce an initial impression and merely add details to enhance your credibility.

Credibility is not a minor thing. The most important thing a client can say to me is that they trust me. Trust comes from credibility. Credibility is the gateway to promotion, advancement, and growth. You establish credibility in several ways—by doing a good job, being reliable, and being truthful. Those are obvious ways. But most people underestimate the power of impressions in establishing credibility.

Women and men have fundamental differences in their nonverbal communication tendencies. In terms of body language, women tend to take up less physical space, sit with their arms and legs towards their body, gesture inwardly, and lean forward when listening. Men on the other hand, take up more physical space, sit with their arms and legs extended, gesture outwardly, and lean backward when listening.

In terms of facial expressions, women tend to look at a person directly, while men tend to tilt their head and look at a person from an angle, not straight on. Women provide more expressions and tend to visually react to what is said more so than men. Men tend to display a frown or even squint when they listen; however, women, regardless of what is being said, tend to smile and nod their head when listening.

During negative interactions or tense moments, men stare while women lower their eyes to avert conflict. As you can see, we are as different as night and day. Women also tend to take verbal rejection more personally, while men take rejection far less personally.

In a culture where the male style of communication and leadership remains the gold standard, it is important to recognize the differences, and revise your actions where improvement is necessary. There is nothing wrong with a few minor enhancements, right?

S.K.I.R.T.S. Strategy Five: SHOW It before You SAY It.   Know that what you do and how you appear matters! Nonverbal communication is important. In fact, it is more important and makes a much stronger, deeper, and longer-lasting impact than verbal communication. You can rarely create trust and confidence with words alone. It is virtually impossible. Your demeanor, eye contact, appearance, and body language will either add to or subtract from your ability to connect meaningfully with your listener. The goal (always!) when speaking in a professional setting is to establish credibility.

For women, credibility is what will make you or break you. To have credibility means that people can rely upon what you say, they believe you, believe *in* you, and trust you. Your nonverbal expression will reveal more about your confidence than words ever could.

My advice is to envision the image that you want to project, and work backwards from there. Spend time in the mirror, and if possible on video camera, assessing your mannerisms. The next time you have a one-on-one conversation in professional setting, pay attention to your eye contact, the firmness of your handshake, your posture, and facial expressions.

Looking people directly in the eyes signifies confidence. And, when you listen, don't nod. Nodding indicates agreement. Be pleasant, but be careful not to smile (or "oversmile") when you want to be taken seriously on a particular manner. Women often try to soften up their messages in an effort to build rapport and maintain relationships. There is nothing inherently wrong with doing this, but balance and timing is important.

So, from your handshake to your hairstyle, make sure you send the right signals.

Our Advantage: The Female Factor

Knowing that men and women are different is half the battle; the other half is calling a truce and emphasizing our strengths rather than wasting time fretting over (perceived) weaknesses. When a big guy fights a small guy, the odds might seem stacked in favor of the larger of the two opponents, but know that in every battle both sides have vast numbers of advantageous resources on which to draw, if only they'll recognize and utilize them.

The larger man may have weight, height, muscle, and brute force on his side, but the smaller man may have speed, agility, stamina, and flexibility on his. If the smaller opponent can outlast the first few initial onslaughts of the larger man, that man may tire and grow exhausted, giving the smaller opponent a decided advantage.

This is not to say that we are the smaller, more limber opponent or to say that we have brute force or bigger size on our side, but only to point out that when it comes to men and women, we have as many strengths as they do—so stop dwelling on the weaknesses. Recognize what makes you powerful and unique and stop apologizing for who, or what, you are. Take your strength back and use what is uniquely yours. In a room full of men, don't see yourself as outnumbered but see it as an opportunity to inject the feminine touch into an otherwise male-dominated atmosphere.

We know this is often easier said than done, but to classify all men as callous brutes who ignore the feminine voice is to stereotype them as they have stereotyped us; we all know the damage of stereotypes.

Instead, trust that one or two men present will have open ears and will encourage you to share your opinion. Fear and intimidation is often the biggest weakness of all, but confidence and knowledge can eliminate that weakness and turn it into a strength. It is all a matter of perspective.

If you think you don't have anything to contribute, you're probably right; if you think you do have something to offer, I know you're right. You have to believe you can communicate effectively first before anyone else can agree with you.

The Needle and Thread: Sewing Your Communication Together

Remember that communication isn't only what you say, but how you say it and even how you look when you say it. Some of my favorite scenes in movies aren't action scenes, special effects, or even romantic kissing scenes, but passionate, emotional, and well-delivered speeches that truly resonate with me personally.

I've even been known to watch a movie a few times and fast-forward to the speech I love the most, like a passionate closing argument in a courtroom scene or a toast at a wedding, just to analyze how the actor delivers the lines.

Good actors, like good speakers, know that there are three elements to communication.

1. *Verbal:* What are you saying? Are the words on target, clear, and concise? Is your message being delivered well? Are you saying what you mean and meaning what you say?

2. *Vocal:* What is your tone? Is it too loud for the words you're saying—or not loud enough? Are you screaming when you should be shouting, shouting when you should be calm, and whispering when you should be firm? Are you in a bad mood, and does it show in your tone of voice?

3. *Visual:* How do you look when you're speaking? Are your visual cues matching your message? In other words, are you frowning when you're delivering good news and smiling when you're giving bad news?

When we speak, most of us are standing on a wobbly stool. What do I mean by that? Let's say a certain stool has three legs; we'll call that stool "communication." Each of the three legs are equally important: we'll call them "verbal," "vocal," and "visual." Since a lot of us worry more about the words than how we'll deliver them or what we'll look like when we're saying them, the verbal aspect of our communication gets longer while the other two legs get smaller; we become wobbly in our delivery.

To see this effect live and in person, watch your local newscasters switch from the tragic story that led to the news to a lighter story about the upcoming holiday weekend or the break in the weather; the transition is often blunt and unpleasant because they're focusing on the words and not realizing that moments after giving bad news they're smiling and upbeat. I know this is a necessary evil, but not where you're concerned.

You can be aware of all three legs of the communication stool by paying equal attention to each part. Simply being aware of how you communicate your message helps you communicate it that much more effectively.

If the stool analogy isn't working for you, you can compare communicating effectively with putting together a dynamite outfit. It's not just the power suit or the silk blouse that matters (verbal), but the accessories you wear to accentuate them (visual), and even how you walk, smile, or act while you're wearing them (vocal).

Walking into a room dressed well and making a good first impression is no different from speaking well and making a good first impression; all the pieces have to not only go together but *flow* together to make it all work.

Have you ever seen someone slouching in a diamond necklace or wearing a silk blouse that's wrinkled? How about someone teetering on $400 heels or swinging their leather purse like a softball bat? Which one of these things is not like the other? When it comes to communication, you can't speak brilliant words without making eye contact or scream a message that is more effective when it's whispered; all legs of the stool— all elements of your power suit—must match so that the message is effective.

The Fitting Room: What Communication Style Suits You?

When it comes to communication, your style is as important as your sentences. Or, as we've learned, how you say something is as important as what you're saying. Failure to recognize this basic truth creates a disconnect when people spend most of their time worrying about the words they'll use, while neglecting how they'll say those words.

It's important to know your communication style. Have you ever watched someone give a presentation, make a quick speech, or simply just rouse a room full of three or four coworkers and thought, "Wow, she really knows how to talk." Typically, this is no accident. The best communicators are aware of the importance of communication, in general, and the value of knowing their communication style, in particular.

It's not different from fashion. We all know what looks good on us, so we tend to wear, *ta dum*, that which looks good on us. I know women whose entire wardrobe is comprised of various combinations of black, white, and red, and others who favor more vibrant hues, ranging from tawny fall colors to eclectic summer aquas and jasmines, but at the end of the day each wears the colors that look good on them, and that's what's important. Have you ever seen someone who simply doesn't know what looks good on them? You can tell immediately; it's what keeps the writers of those "Worst Dressed Lists" occupied during the days and weeks after the Oscars or the Golden Globes.

When a person uses the wrong communication style, mixes styles, or simply ignores styles, the same thing happens; there should be a "Worst Stressed List" because these people stress the wrong message at the wrong time, speak too loudly when they should go soft, or speak too softly when they should be loud. Are you on the Worst Stressed List? Find out by analyzing your communication style in the following list.

◆ *Assertive:* The assertive speaker is cool and confident; she says what she means and means what she says. She has good ideas and is not afraid to share them, either in private, one-on-one conversations or in front of groups. She has learned to speak her mind appropriately, not aggressively (see the following for an explanation of the difference), and knows the value of listening that is appropriate, as well. Her assertive communication style can make her a true asset to the organization.

◆ *Aggressive:* We all speak to an agenda; typically that agenda is not personal (at least, not at work). The aggressive speaker often talks to a more personal than professional agenda, in my experience, as she often finds it hard to differentiate between the two. Her words can be catty and off-color, and offend as often as they inspire. Instead of speaking to inspire or share knowledge, as the assertive speaker does—and as the passive speaker tries to—the aggressive speaker often talks to shape or solidify an agenda. Her presence in the workplace can be damaging if she is given too many opportunities to speak.

◆ *Passive-Aggressive:* The passive-aggressive speaker hides her true aggression by often playing the "good girl" role. She'll speak quietly, even softly, and use temperate, lukewarm words, all the while issuing orders or making "suggestions" that undermine your authority and put you at odds with the rest of the staff. While she may make a better impression than the aggressive speaker, her words can be just as damaging in the long run as her passivity gives way to her true aggression.

♦ *Passive:* The passive speaker is the polar opposite of the assertive speaker, which is why you'll find them at opposite ends of the spectrum. Where the assertive speaker talks from confidence and poise, the passive speaker talks from a place of shyness or reserve. Her messages often get lost in the "ums" and "ahs" that dot her speech, and while she may have brilliant ideas or helpful hints to share with the rest of the office, few will stick around long enough to hear them because her delivery lacks force.

Body Language: The Missing Link

You can make a great mixed drink with just the right ingredients, top it off with just enough pineapple slices or lemon wedges, and go to the trouble of using crushed ice instead of cubed, but if you pour it into a three-year-old juice glass with chipped edges, how much of a presentation do you think it's going to make?

That's a little like what happens when you go to the trouble of carefully choosing your words, matching your vocal tone to your visual delivery, but ruin all of these with body language that doesn't quite match up.

Body language is different from the visual aspect of your communication style. When we speak of communicating visually, we're more concerned with whether our facial expression is matching up to our delivery; smiling instead of frowning, blinking too often, entering the room with a scowl, and so on.

Body language means the whole enchilada.

♦ *Posture:* All those times your parents told you to "sit up straight" or "keep your chin up" might have been good advice after all. Your posture can say what your eyes, lips, tongue, and brain cannot; it can assure people, warn people, enlighten people, and frighten people. How you walk into a room often determines your actions to follow. If you walk in with you head up, smiling, on the balls of your feet, shoulders straight, and back firm, chances are that everyone in the room will notice and mimic you accordingly. Conversely, if you slouch in, slump down into your chair, and do your best to sink back into the ground, your actions will help derail the meeting in no time flat.

♦ *Demeanor:* Your demeanor is born inside and radiates outward; the physical can affect the mental. Even if you're feeling bad, perking up, stretching, breathing, or even smiling can literally change your entire mood. According to the British Dental Health Foundation, "a smile gives the same level of stimulation as eating 2,000 chocolate bars. The results were found after scientists measured brain and heart activity in volunteers as they were shown pictures of smiling people and given money and chocolate."

♦ *Accessibility:* Is your body language sending out the wrong signals? Be cautious of how you stand, sit, or simply just go about your daily activities. The way you stand, cock your head, spread your legs, square your shoulders, or even tap your toes can welcome people—or shut them down. You have to be accessible to be approachable; your body is the gateway that either opens or closes your accessibility.

♦ *Sign language:* Crossing your arms can ward people off; opening them can welcome people. Tapping your pen can indicate frustration or distrust; licking your lips, tossing your hair, and rolling your eyes are all aspects of sign language that send signals you may not want to be transmitting. Be alert to your little daily tics and see how they affect people. If you're someone who says as much with her body as she does with her words, make sure those signals, signs, and messages are the right ones, not the wrong ones.

♦ *Tone:* Did you know that your body language can signal, alert, drive, or even change the entire tone of a conversation? Body language is extremely powerful; how you stand, walk, move your arms, or even sit can send off messages that are both undermining and overwhelming to your verbal communication. Be aware of all of the above points to ensure that you don't send the wrong tone with your body.

Lessons for M.E. (Motivation and Empowerment)

The bottom line with communication is that the more passionate we are about what we have to say, the fewer hang-ups we'll have about saying it in the first place. It's easy to get caught up in the *how* of doing something; how to stand firm and deliver your message effectively and always with a smile. But it's important to remember that the *how* is only a way to get to the *why*.

Why do we need to communicate more effectively? To add value, to earn respect, to move the organization—and our careers—forward.

Why do we want to say this particular thing? Because it's important to us, because it adds value, because we're the right person to say it at the right time.

This entire chapter has been about the *how*; only you can determine the *why*. And the why makes it all the more easier, let me tell you. I always find a *why* when I prepare a presentation, either to one client at a time or a boardroom full of executives.

Why do I want to sign Ima Hooper? Because she's a woman of value and vision and I know I'm the right person to help her dream big dreams and gain great ground. Now I can speak to her with passion and power.

Why do I want Sparks Soda to endorse Ima? Because they are an upstart, underdog company who bucked the system and competed with Coke and Pepsi to earn hard-won market share in a cutthroat market. Their messages are synergistic and I know that, with the right campaign, both can come out on top. Now I can deliver that message uniquely and effectively because I know so powerfully *what it is*.

Remember that communication is, first and foremost, a means to convey a message. It's easy to get so caught up in the delivery—what to say, how to say it, what to wear, and how to look when saying it—that the message gets lost. That's why the most effective communicators are the ones who share the message so directly; it's not lost in pyrotechnics and five-dollar words you have to write down and look up when you get home to understand.

I have been fortunate enough to bear witness to many great communicators in my lifetime. Some have been in front of large classrooms, others in front of small denominations in modest churches; some have been onstage or in the country's most televised boardrooms—regardless, it was not the setting or the scenery or the suit that impressed me so much as the simplicity and power of the *message.*

Try it and see; the worksheet that follows is one of the most effective tools I've found for whittling down the mass hysteria to get to the message. You can also find more valuable information at www.skirt sintheboardroom.com. Use it and communication will be one more valuable tool you will use o your way to becoming S.K.I.R.T.S.-savvy.

Set No Limits Reflection

Have you ever left a meeting, conference call, workshop, or seminar and wondered "What was the speaker's message?" If you did, then the speaker was one in name only; he or she probably wasn't a great messenger. That's because great communication starts with the message first.

Ask any great mystery writer and she'll tell you that you've got to know the ending before you start at the beginning. I mean, you can't leave clues and drop hints about the killer for 300 or more pages *if you don't know who the killer is*! Solve the mystery before you open your mouth; know the message before you become the messenger. Now, you don't have to be giving the keynote at Microsoft's Employee Appreciation Day for the exercise below to work. This is as true for simple, day-to-day communication—coworker to colleague, boss to employee, department to department—as it is for bigger meetings or even corporate events.

It all boils down to my three-part A.S.K. Strategy: Assign Importance, Separate the Wheat from the Chaff, and Know Your Main Talking Point.

PART ONE: ASSIGN IMPORTANCE

For a message to be clear, it must be concise. We often think more is more; when it comes to messages leaving a lasting impression, less is more. Whether you are going to ask for a raise, suggest a new idea to the marketing department, interview for a job, or write ad copy for your new product, focus on what's *most* important, not *all* that's important.

For years, Hallmark has had the same message: "When you care enough to send the very best." It's smart, calculated, on point, and on target. You immediately equate Hallmark with the best; that's the message. And there are just enough keywords in there—care, send—to let you know they're talking about sending greeting cards through the mail.

Now, here's what that message might have sounded like in the hands of a poor communicator: "When the person you care about is important enough for you to send a card to, send one of our sensitive cards so that they will feel important and also loved, revered, respected, etc." Do you see the difference? While the second slogan contains more keywords and is more specific and detailed, its message is weakened *because* of the fact that it contains more keywords and is more specific and detailed.

Now then, when you have a vague message you want to deliver, narrow it down by zeroing in on three main talking points to explore as you communicate.

1. _____

2. _____

3. _____

PART TWO: SEPARATE THE WHEAT FROM THE CHAFF

We started this exercise with three main ideas; now we need to whittle that down to two that you can focus in on and finally zero in on your main talking point. On the two lines below, eliminate one of the three main ideas from above:

1. _____

2. _____

PART THREE: KNOW YOUR MAIN TALKING POINT

Now that you've *a*ssigned importance and *s*eparated the wheat from the chaff, use the space below to isolate your single main talking point.

1. _____

Sample A.S.K. Strategy Worksheet

For a little extra guidance, here's an example of a worksheet that illustrates how I might have gone about applying the A.S.K. Strategy for my fictional client, Ima Hooper:

PART ONE: ASSIGN IMPORTANCE

I want Ima Hooper to know why we are the right team to work together. I don't want to give her an avalanche of information in our coffee-shop meeting, so I want to pare my message down to the most salient details. I think those are:

1. I can help you broaden your awareness in the public eye via my marketing experience.

2. I can connect you with foundations and charitable organizations so you can do more good.

3. I can help you be a more effective and enthusiastic speaker to help spread your message.

PART TWO: SEPARATE THE WHEAT FROM THE CHAFF

As I research Ima more, I really get a sense that her passion and commitment to charitable organizations is more important to her than becoming a household name or selling feminine products. So that enables me to "separate the wheat from the chaff" and narrow my talking points down even further.

1. I can connect you with foundations and charitable organizations so you can do more good.

2. I can help you be a more effective and enthusiastic speaker to help spread your message.

PART THREE: KNOW YOUR MAIN TALKING POINT

I know that if I can hold Ima's interest and get her talking to me, I can convince her that being marketed better helps her start more foundations and raise more money for charities, but first I need to convince her that I'm as passionate about foundations and charities as she is—and that I know as much about them as I can. I also know that getting Ima to be more comfortable speaking to crowds is an important, but optional, skill set that we can cover when we're partners. For now, I know my main talking point should be:

1. I can connect you with foundations and charitable organizations so you can do more good.

Chapter 6

Connections

Do Shorter Skirts Ever Hurt?

Con•nec•tion (*n*) a relationship or important association; united by kinship or common interests.

Many say that it is "who you know" that determines where you go. Ladies, that is only partially true. Ultimately, where you go is about your ability to expand upon "who you know" by networking. Plus, it is about how *well* you know "who you know," what the "who you know" say about you, *and* how much the "who you know" trusts you. Most people think about networking as a numbers game. In essence, they try to meet as many people as possible to get as much as they need as possible. That's the wrong approach! True networking is about quality, not quantity. Anyone can collect a ton of business cards, just like a man can collect a stack of phone numbers—maybe he can't collect yours, but that is precisely my point! Quality, not quantity, counts.

Networking is the process of establishing quality relationships. I define quality relationships as relationships filled with value. Without an exchange of value, there can be no true relationship. An employer and employee have a relationship. The employee gives time and effort to the employer. The employer gives compensation to the employee. There is an exchange. Likewise, a customer and a company have a relationship. The customer gives money to the company. The company gives a product or service to the customer. Think of your closest personal friendships. There is mutual exchange of value there as well. You give your time and attention to your best friend, and your best friend likely gives you the same thing in return.

Relationships (exchanges of value) are everywhere. So, to maximize your networking, you must realize two very important things. First, you must realize your value. What do you have to offer? What do you know that others need to know? How can you enrich someone else's life? How can you enhance someone else's professional growth? All of these add to your value.

Second, you must know what you need. What is it that would be valuable to you in return? Think about where you are versus where you want to be. Who and what do you need to know and have in order to arrive at your destination? Herein lays the ultimate purpose of networking: *To find synergies that will advance mutual interests and open new opportunities.*

Networking is a give-and-take process. Notice that the word *give* comes first, not the word *take.* You only get as much as you give. The more you give of yourself, your time, and your expertise, the more others will want to assist you as well. Think of your relationships as a chain. Every time you extend yourself, you form a link to another person. When that person returns the favor, you've now linked together and have formed a connection. The more you mutually assist each other, the tighter and stronger the chain becomes. That's what makes a good network. If you only take as opposed to giving, then you become the weak link. And remember that the weak link is always disposable.

Building a solid, sincere network (a multifaceted, interwoven set of connections) will enable you to expand your associations. You'll also stay connected to the new wave of industry trends, and make connections for future opportunities—personal and professional. These relationships occur on multiple levels every day. I believe it requires you to be at the right POINT, with the right POSTURE, and in the right PLACE. Let's explore how you can work your S.K.I.R.T. and make your net *work.*

Each contact with a human being is so rare, so precious, one should preserve it.

—Anais Nin

The Right POINT: Contacts versus Connections

When building your network, it is important to remember that you have three points of contact with others: past (old), present (current), and potential (future) contacts. Each of these is equally important. However, if you focus on developing only one area, you'll fail to grow your network in a solid and substantial manner.

PAST

If you focus only on past contacts, you're limiting your ability to move forward. Furthermore, you'll be likely to miss changing trends and access to resources that will be necessary to take your career or your business to the next level.

PRESENT

Present contacts are extremely important because they represent your *now*. If you neglect your current contacts, then you stand to tarnish your reputation. Most of my new business comes through referrals from my current clients and contacts in my current network. I have to take care of and maintain them. However, if you *only* focus on present contacts, then you are again limiting your growth.

POTENTIAL

The future can be exciting because it holds endless possibilities. The danger, however, in focusing on only the future is that you neglect the present, which can damage your reputation for reliability. People will think that you're only concerned with the next best thing. There is no trust or loyalty in people who only focus on the future. I see sports agents who do this all of the time. They focus on the next big superstar while neglecting their current clients. This is what motivated me to get into the sports industry—to fill a gap by providing quality and comprehensive service to the "now" clientele of players.

Whenever I leave a meeting—especially one where I meet a lot of people—I divide my business cards into three stacks: stack one: Potential; stack two: No Potential; and stack three: Not Sure. The people you meet will fall into one of these three categories as well. You'll have contacts who present the potential for future interaction, contacts who present no potential at all whatsoever, and contacts who leave you with no sense of direction.

When you meet people, *you* will fall into one of those three categories as well. If you're networking for the purpose of going somewhere, you want to fall into stack one—the one filled with potential—at the right time, and the right place. You cannot always end up in stack one, and you shouldn't. You have to remain focused on who you are and what you're about, so that you do not spread yourself too thin, and, in the process dilute your value. (We will talk about personal branding later in the chapter on captivation).

Pulling Your Past, Present, and Potential Contacts Together

Regardless of whether you are maintaining or growing past, present, or potential contacts, all networking is about quality, not quantity. When I first moved to Washington, D.C., straight out of college, I attended a seminar. The lecturer gave me one piece of advice that was good, but not great. He told the audience that being in Washington, D.C., would open up a wide array of opportunities if you make the effort to expand your network. Specifically, he said, your influence is only as strong as your Rolodex is thick. That really stuck with me. I realized then, as a college student in a new place filled with power-players and power-brokers, that I would need to know more than just my roommates, and more than just the people in that auditorium. Now, as years have gone by, I realize that his piece of advice was missing one key ingredient. He emphasized the importance of *meeting* new people, but failed to touch on the importance of truly *knowing* people. There is a huge difference.

At ME Unlimited, our agency is called upon to conduct a wide array of performance strategy trainings at conferences across the country. On any given day, I can meet hundreds of people. I can even collect hundreds of business cards, e-mail addresses, and phone numbers. However, I can meet hundreds of people without making one connection. A business card in and of itself holds no value. If the person you reach out to on the business card does not know you (or get to know you), the card is simply taking up space. A business card is only valuable if it serves as a gateway to future collaboration and interaction of some sort.

At any given time, I'm reviewing old e-mails and sifting through old business cards to follow-up with past contacts. I'm making sure that I maintain and deliver for my present contacts. And I'm constantly networking, meeting new people, and looking for ways to grow the business by seeking out potential contacts. As much as I take time to nurture my existing clients base and existing contacts, I have to dedicate substantial time to growing my future client base as well. If took me almost nine months to land my first major NFL client. Nine months is a long time when bills are due every month! In my world, business is very personal, meaning that I have to establish a personal connection and trusting relationship to acquire (and keep) a client. It doesn't happen overnight. Rarely do I meet with someone one time and land their business the same day. It takes time, attention, and follow-up.

Making connections is about truly knowing people. Connections are important for two reasons. *Number one, quality connections expand your influence and your capacity.* Each person I know represents an independent network of contacts, influences, and opportunities. Let's say I'm recruiting a professional athlete who is mostly interested in securing more endorsements. I might have business cards at Nike, Reebok, Under Armor, and Adidas (all major sports apparel companies). However, my capacity to deliver for my client depends on how well I know people at each of these companies. If I know someone really well at each of these places, then I have exponentially expanded my influence in my industry and my capacity to deliver for my client. Can you imagine if I had only the main 1-800 number that the general public uses? Yikes! Having contacts without a connection is like having the 1-800 number. Remember that!

Number two, quality connections advance your career, not just your job. A job and a career are two different things. If you work for a company, you should be building your reputation internally along with your connections externally. No job is ever 100 percent secure. Quality connections become somewhat of a safety blanket, enabling you to have options if something goes wrong, or if you decide to pursue another opportunity. Didn't Mama always say to never put all your eggs in one basket? That principle applies to your network as well. Always build and grow your reputation and connections outside of your job. Entrepreneurs, business owners, and those in sales know this principle very well. You cannot survive without expanding your database of quality connections. Otherwise, your current well will run dry. You must make it a point to fill up with new connections on a regular basis. And a savvy S.K.I.R.T. will go a long way to make a special effort to balance her past, present, and potential points of contacts to build a healthy and helpful network.

The Right POSTURE: AAA Membership Has Its Benefits

I think of networking like I think of success. It is a journey and a process, not a destination. You should constantly be in a state of expanding your network. You do not have to go to a formal networking event, a conference, or on a business trip to meet people who can advance your careers and your opportunity. I spend a lot of time at the airport and on a plane. So I often meet potential clients or contacts at the airport, at a restaurant, a hotel, in the line to the ladies room . . . anywhere. The key is not *where* you are, it is *how* you are. How are you when you're out and about? Are you open and engaging, or closed off and reserved? In additional to being at the right point and positioning yourself in the right *place*, you also have to have the right *posture*. What I mean is that you must be a triple A—Approachable, Assertive, and Astute.

Approachable

In conducting business development seminars for women, I always ask women to ask themselves how they think their friends and colleagues would describe them. Then I ask them to ask their friends and colleagues and see if their perceptions actually match their intentions. It is very important to be approachable in business. I think that, as women, we often feel that we have to be cold or standoffish to impress people or to demonstrate our strength and confidence. Not true. I had to learn this the hard way. I grew up as an individual competitor in individual sports and activities, not team sports and group activities. I was a baton twirler and competed at national and international competitions. My performance was my responsibility. If my performance was not up to par, it was my fault, not a team member's. There was no team! As a team of one, I used to prepare for competition by focusing on my own and blocking out other things and people that could be a distraction.

This style of mental preparation carried over into my adult and professional life. It is not a bad thing, per se. My ability to focus helped me to get through law school and do well in high-pressure situations in court. However, I learned that focus without inclusion can alienate others from your world. You and I both need other people. I've said before that you might be in your business for yourself, but you are never by yourself. Other people are a necessary component of your success. As leader of your own business, or of your career, and no matter where you stand in a team, you must be approachable.

Approachability is (in large part) a matter of body language and demeanor. Standing with your arms crossed all the time isn't going to help you advance your interests; it will hamper you. Smile at people, say hello, be engaging, make eye contact, and acknowledge people when they walk by. As I give this advice, I must admit that being approachable is a learned habit for me, not a natural one. I am extremely independent and self-reliant. I also realized (because I'm told this on a regular basis) that I can come across as intimidating and aloof to some people. This is not my intention, but this is the perception. Perception is reality. So I make a concerted effort to engage other people when I am out of my house and out of my office. As the President and CEO of EDGE 3M Sports & Entertainment, I'm also the Chief Brand Ambassador and Chief Networking Agent for our company. It is largely my personality and ability that bring in celebrity and pro athlete clients. My company has grown immensely because of approachability. Making approachability a priority will boost and build your career as well.

ASSERTIVE

One of the biggest fallacies is that the best things come to those who wait. That's a lie, lie, lie! The best things come to those who hustle! I've said before that to WANT is to Wait And Nothing Transpires. You have to create opportunities by being proactive, and the same holds true with networking. In addition to being approachable, you must also be willing to approach others. You need to be assertive, not aggressive, in expanding your network. I think assertiveness is a by-product of confidence. Be confident in who you are and what you have to offer. From there, know what it is you want to say and how you want to say it. Recently, I was at the airport during a leisure trip. In the security line, I spotted a very famous hip-hop music artist behind me. I knew of this artist's immense popularity, and also his potential to really expand his brand. It also helped that the artist lived in Atlanta, which is where my agency is based. So, I immediately thought about what I would want to say if I had the opportunity to introduce myself and my company. It turned out that the artist and his management team were on my flight! While I was sitting and waiting to board, the artist actually walked by. I smiled. He smiled. I confidently looked him in the eye, addressed him by his name, and asked how he was doing. That started a very productive conversation about his imaging, PR needs, branding, and endorsements. As soon as I introduced myself, I told him that I was an entertainment attorney. (I always establish credibility as soon as possible, which is very important for women in male-dominated fields). He mentioned that he noticed me earlier in the security line and had planned to ask me to be in a music video. Uh . . . no thank you! However, he immediately noticed my professionalism and wanted to discuss the business of his personal branding. In fact, he said, "I can tell that you're smart and sharp. We need to talk further."

If I had just let the artist walk by, I would have never made a point of connection for a potential business opportunity. And even if he had approached me and asked me about the silly music video opportunity (not silly in general, but it's just not the reason why I went to law school), I still needed to be assertive enough to guide and shift the direction of the conversation. People can assume all they want, but they only know what *you* tell them. Be strategic in the information you share. Strategic and relevant information sharing will advance your interests while creating a tighter nexus and focus for your conversations when you meet people. Assertive women know who they are and what they want. Have a picture (metaphorically speaking) of yourself and what your success looks like.

When someone tries to draw you outside your boundaries, be assertive enough to bring them back into the frame. Your success is a canvas on which only you can paint.

ASTUTE

Have you ever meet a know-it-all? Someone who seems to know everything? Well, you do not have to be a know-it-all, but you should be a know-a-lot! You should know your industry, know yourself, and know your brand. When you know what you're talking about, it instills confidence in others and attracts them to you. When you meet people, they can tell if you know what you're talking about. If you know what you're talking about, you're more likely to land a follow-up conversation or meeting. The last element of AAA membership is making sure that you're on top of your game.

In order to be properly equipped and ready you need a few things. First, you need to know your business inside and out. Regardless of whether you are a business owner, an executive, or climbing the corporate ladder at your job, you need to understand your industry or the industry you want to venture into.

When you meet someone the first thing that person will probably ask you what you do. So, the second thing you need is a prepared explanation of your work and what you do. When people ask me what I do, I have two answers ready. Answer 1: I'm an entertainment attorney and own a media, marketing, and branding agency specializing in professional athletes and entertainers. Answer 2: I'm an attorney and I actually own two companies. ME Unlimited focuses on performance strategy, and EDGE 3M is a media, marketing, and branding agency focused on professional athletes and entertainers. Which answer I give is predicated on the circumstances and whom I'm meeting. If I'm going to a sports combine, I won't even bring up ME Unlimited. It's irrelevant information for the environment. In almost any other nonsport, non-celebrity, or nonentertainment setting, I'll go with answer number two. I give myself two avenues for potential synergy to develop. Maybe they want to hire ME Unlimited to conduct a corporate seminar. Or maybe that person knows a professional athlete that needs branding. Or maybe there is no synergy at all! But by having your information together about yourself and your industry, you position yourself to move the conversation further.

Third, you need to understand and be able to clearly communicate how your profession can help others. When someone meets you and you explain your industry, you should explain it in the context of the value you and your company add. That's how you discover synergy and opportunities for future business. When I met the hip-hop artist at the airport, I introduced myself and my company, but I also framed the introduction by sharing information about how we help celebrities and athletes elevate their brand. I didn't spend a lot of time talking about our media and graphic services, but I didn't think that would be a strong need area where additional work could develop. Not in that instance. However, I did know that our marketing and endorsement procurement services would be of interest, so I focused on that area. Most people introduce themselves without giving thought to what they want say. The lesson here is to know your stuff!

The Right PLACE: The Four Phases of Networking

It can be critically important to be in the right place at the right time. Networking can happen anywhere. In fact, if you join me at the S.K.I.R.T.S. in the Boardroom: Set No Limits Summit, you'll meet some of the most dynamic businesswomen in the country. I want us to close this section on networking by outlining the four phases of networking. Again, networking is a process! It happens in four phases: Mingling, Mating, Meeting, and Matching. (See Figure 6.1.) Let's explore each phase together.

Phase One: *Mingling*

In the first phase of networking you simply meet people. You're most effective in phase one if you can clearly communicate three things: (1) what you do, (2) what you need, and (3) what value you bring to the table. It's like going to the grocery store and writing a shopping list before you arrive. There is a lot to choose from in the store, so having a predetermined outline of what you do, what you need to advance, and what you bring to the table will focus your search. Mingling should not

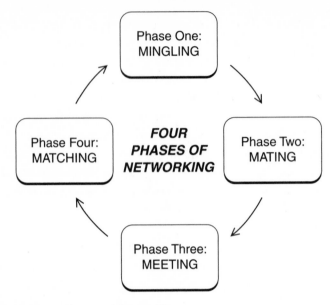

FIGURE **6.1** The Four Phases of Networking

be too in-depth; it is an initial opportunity to establish a connection in which there are potential mutually beneficial synergies. After mingling, the goal is to follow up with your strongest leads, and to maintain contact with other potentials leads, as well.

PHASE TWO: *MATING*

In the second phase of networking, playfully called mating, you begin somewhat of a courting process with the potential contact. This is done with a follow-up phone call or e-mail to let the potential contact know of your interest in learning more about his or her business. At this time you should be more clear about and more detailed in your objectives and your abilities to add value to the other person's profession. The more you can add value, the more interesting you become. Do not focus as much on what you need, but focus more on areas of synergies.

PHASE THREE: *MEETING*

In the third phase of networking, meeting, you dedicate time to exploring specific opportunities and desired outcomes. Before going to a meeting, you should use the information you've gathered from the mingling and mating phases to shape your goals and objectives for the face-to-face or one-on-one meeting. It does not matter whether the meeting happens over the phone or in person. What is important is that you have a plan for what you would like to see accomplished, along with a specific pitch strategy for yourself, your service, your product, or your company. Don't be afraid to state clearly what you would like to see happen moving forward. That includes listing what you will commit to do, and what you would like to see in return. Always leave a meeting with a clear and concise understanding of the next steps moving forward.

PHASE FOUR: *MATCHING*

In the fourth and final phase of networking, matching, you begin to take action steps towards implementation. Based on the game plan established during the meeting phase, you need to have a clear roadmap for how you plan to fulfill your end of the expectation bargain. It is very important to be able to deliver on what you promise. The best ideas and the greatest of intentions mean nothing without follow-through. You must be timely. You must be accurate. And you must deliver quality work. By doing so, you gain the confidence and trust of your new contact. Trust is what makes your network work!

Top Five Networking Nudges: Things You Should Do

Now that you know the phases of networking, here are a few tips to keep in mind as you go through the process. As with anything else in life, the more you practice, the better you become.

1. *Avoid Stuck-up Selecting.* Be careful not to talk with only those individuals you think are important and can help you. The truth of the matter is that you never know where the best contacts may come from. Be friendly, open, and engaging with people in general, and you'll find that you increase your network with a diverse array of contacts and key connections.

2. *Value People.* Understand that everyone you meet has value and something to offer. The truth of the matter is, most of the people whom you meet may not be able to help you. But you may be able to help them. As a result, you may be planting positive seeds that will come to fruition. Quite often I get business referrals from people who are nowhere close to being in my industry. However, if I've treated a person with respect, kindness, and generosity, then that person becomes more likely to refer you when someone else in their network might be in need of someone like you.

3. *Socialize.* Get out of the house. And get out of your office. You cannot meet people if you are in the middle of the action. You can meet people casually at networking mixers and happy hours. If you carry your professional game face with you everywhere you go, you make professional connections anywhere! I got into the world of professional sports at the airport. I make *a lot* of connections on airplanes, and have gotten some great business leads at the hair salon. The key is to be engaging (as I've said before) with others, and to have a clear and compelling picture of what you do, what you need, and what you bring to the table. You can socialize more strategically by joining associations and professional groups, and by attending conferences, workshops, and seminars.

4. *K.I.S.S. 'E.M.* *K*eep *I*t *S*uper *S*imple, *E*asy, and *M*anageable. Make it easy for someone to help you. Often times when people meet a new contact, they ask for too much too soon. You do not want to overwhelm someone with your ideas and plans. Also, you do not want to ask for too much. You'll scare someone away before you finish your first sentence. I recommend starting small with simple things that establish trust and a solid foundation for a future, more substantial working relationship. A colleague of mine and I went to meet with a large company that was interested in expanding its franchise operations. We had an excellent first meeting with the company. In fact the meeting was almost too good. We discussed perhaps a dozen potential ideas and ways that we could help the company. While that sounds good, a dozen ideas is too many. We decided to focus on our top three strongest service areas (the ones

we knew we could ace), and then go back to the company so it could choose its top priority. We wanted them to pick one thing that we could focus on and deliver with excellence. By doing so, we made it easy on ourselves to make a good impression. And we also made it easy for the company to give us a chance.

5. *Be Ready.* Always be ready for new opportunities to come your way. Women who *expect* to succeed also expect to meet the people they need to know in order to make their vision a reality. As such, you should always have you're A-game ready. As I mentioned, you could meet the one person who elevates your career to the next level anywhere. So always have your business cards. Always have your professional introduction of yourself (your spill) ready to go. And, wherever you go and whatever you do, present yourself with confidence, class, and charisma.

Work Your S.K.I.R.T.S. from the Inside-Out

At the end of the day, networking can be one of the most effective tools for enhancing your career. One of the best pieces of advice that I received from a coworker at my former law firm was this: You have your job, but you also have your career. Take the time to develop *both*. Remember that networking can happen on two levels: internally (inside the work environment) and externally (outside the work environment). Developing your internal network will help you advance within your job. Think of your internal network as individuals and opportunities to grow within your company and climb the corporate ladder rung-by-rung. On the other hand, developing your external network expands the depth, width, and diverse scope of your overall career opportunities. Think of your external network as an actual net. The more substantive contacts you have, the wider and stronger your net. So, if you do decide to change companies or change careers, you have options. Many women stay in their current jobs because they feel like they do not have any other options. The reality is that you have to create options for yourself. The best things do not come to those who wait! You must build a bridge *before* you need to cross it, and dig your well *before* you're thirsty. That's the value of external networking.

Thus far, I've focused largely on external networking, or networking outside of your job. For those of you who are nonbusiness owners and have a job, remember that networking happens internally within your company as well. It is perfectly fine to have friends in the workplace. However, avoid joining a clique. Cliques, by their very nature, often exclude others. I think of a clique as a closed and rigid circle that forms prematurely. The circle never has a true chance to expand and reach its ultimate shape and fullest potential because it has stopped growing too soon. By associating solely with a limited group of people, you cap your growth potential as well. As women, we have to be particularly sensitive to avoiding cliques. Meet people at a variety of different levels within your company, and make your presence known without being pushy or too obvious. The best way to have an impact is to have a positive attitude, to be approachable, and to deliver quality work on every occasion. Take time to apply these networking principles to develop your potential at your job and to develop your career as a whole. There is tremendous value in developing your internal and external network. Every savvy S.K.I.R.T. should make sure to do both.

Lessons for M.E. (Motivation and Empowerment)

Networking is the process of establishing quality relationships—that is, relationships that are filled with value. Without an exchange of value, there can be no true relationship. Relationships (exchanges of value) are everywhere. Plus, it's not just "who you know" that determines where you go. You must expand "who you know" by networking and creating a true network of people who *know* and *trust* you.

When building your network, you must focus on your three points of contact: past (old), present (current), and potential (future) contacts. Furthermore, pay careful attention to enhancing your internal and external networking skills so that you can grow within your job while constantly keeping your overall career options open as well. Do not focus on developing on one area alone, or you'll fail to grow your network in a solid and substantial manner.

Set No Limits Reflection

Networking is on-going process. Just like a garden, you have to nurture it so that it can grow. Let's examine how you can nurture your network. What is my personal sound-bite introduction? (Focus on what you do and make it interesting, but also keep it short and sweet.)

_____

_____

_____

_____

What value do I bring to the table? (Focus on your Talents, Abilities, Gifts, and Skills. Highlight one to three deliverables that make you unique in your field.)

_____

_____

_____

_____

What do I need to advance? (Focus on the type of people, resources, skills, and opportunities you need to align yourself with in order to advance your job growth and your career.)

Internal Networking Needs: Your Job

_____

_____

_____

_____

_____

External Networking Needs: Your Career

_____

_____

_____

_____

_____

Chapter 7

Creativity

Show 'Em Your Assets

Crea•tivi•ty (*n*) having the ability or power to create

When Isabelle "Izzy" Tihanyi first began surfing at the age of eight, she probably never dreamed she could one day found a company centered around her love of surfing. But years later, that's exactly what she did. She joined her twin sister, Caroline "Coco" Tihanyi, and the two surf divas created a company called, appropriately enough, Surf Divas.

Originally the company began by doing something the twins knew best: teaching surfing, primarily to women and young girls. As their success grew, however, the men naturally wanted in on the act; now Surf Divas caters to both men and women, young and old, but that's not all. The company now features a full line of bikinis and surf wear; accessories such as key chains, flip-flops, and sunglasses; and even a book, *Surf Diva: A Girl's Guide to Getting Good Waves*.

Asked about the company's good fortunes on its ten-year anniversary, sisters Izzy and Coco summed up their success thus: "It's about fun, being together, and meeting so many cool people!" No doubt, but you and I both know that succeeding in business is about a lot more than that. If there's one recurring theme I noticed while learning more about Surf Divas, it was the creativity behind not only the Surf Divas name but just about everything the two original surf divas touched.

From the company web site to the book cover to the design logo to the photo galleries featuring sun-baked surf-worshippers, the company's image screamed their unique mission statement: "It's about fun, being together, and meeting so many cool people!"

I would add "creativity" to this list.

Creativity is underestimated, underappreciated and undervalued. But it's more powerful than you might think. In fact, creativity is what moves most choices. Think about it. Most decisions are made at an emotional level, and then later rationalized intellectually later. That is why you can buy something because you "wanted" it, but later you either regret or rejoice based on whether you actually "needed" it.

In business your ability to add value to a company or a consumer is based largely on your creativity—the extent to which your thoughts add value. For example, consultants add value by thinking about new strategies. A company hires a new CEO to think about effective ways to strengthen the company's efforts and energy. A manager is hired to think about efficiency and execution.

In business, we were traditionally taught that creativity was a soft skill, something difficult to measure on a spreadsheet come the end of the fourth quarter. In other words, creativity is optional, maybe even nice, but far from necessary. But a new wave of thinking, consulting, and leading has taught us that a creative thinker is an ingenious, inventive, and innovative problem solver. In short, creativity is an organizational asset in every way imaginable.

Are you creative? Ask yourself:

- Do I love what I do?
- Am I thinking about it, even when I'm off the clock?
- Am I able to use my creativity at work?
- Do I see creativity as a necessity or a luxury?
- Am I rewarded for my creativity in my workplace?
- Is there more I could be doing, creatively, to add value to my company?
- Have I been recognized for my creativity?
- Would I like to be?

Creativity is your fingerprint, your spin, your spice, your salt 'n' pepper, your touch, your input, your insight, and your intellect. It's *you*. Essentially, creativity is your ability not only to think, but to think uniquely.

Creativity, in its best form, emerges when you embrace Y.O.U., or *Your Own Uniqueness*. Creativity is the thing that only *you* have; therefore, there is an inherent value that only *you* can offer. Think of your ideas and your ability to add value to any given circumstance with your perspective as a missing piece to the puzzle. Not just any piece, *the* piece—the piece that not only makes it complete, but immensely better. When it comes to your creativity, it is important that you embrace it so that you can unlock it.

Creativity is what made Ben & Jerry's more than just another brand of ice cream. Creativity is what made Martha Stewart more than just a purveyor of "good things." Creativity is what made Oprah more than just another talk show host. Creativity is what enabled me to lead Donald Trump's team of women to our only win against the men on *The Apprentice*.

Whenever sports clients come to our branding agency to build their personal brand, they are looking for something different and unique. They do not want to blend in. Brands do not blend in, they burst out. Each client that walks in the door has the ability to "burst" into the marketplace. Our job is to craft a comprehensive, outside-the-box strategy to make that happen.

My philosophy is that if you want something that you have never had, you have to be willing to do something you have never done. . . *and* do something that no one else can do or will do. That's the expectation when we start brainstorming. It's like trying on a new outfit that you never knew would fit. If it's the right idea, it'll fit perfectly.

So what makes something the right idea? Well, the right idea is always relative; if it's just not *you*, it's never going to be right for you no matter how right it is for somebody else. It depends on all of the circumstances; all of the unique qualities you bring to the brainstorming session. However, there are five key elements to creativity and using it to enhance your professional life:

1. *Originality.* Creativity is not fake. Your creativity should reflect an authentic, sincere, and real you. It should be an expression of what you think, what you feel, and what you dream. Not a copy of what someone else is doing or a copy of some fad that, by the time you

get around to it, will already be done and gone. Innovative companies, and successful women who rapidly accelerate their careers, are those who stay ahead of the trend. Copycats can only play catch up. Set the trend. Better yet, *be* the trend.

2. *Imagination.* As I tell my clients all the time, "You can't be creative on autopilot." Your creativity requires an active element of dreaming, brainstorming, thinking bigger, better, and bolder. You have to push the envelope. As we say at EDGE 3M, "If you are not living on the EDGE, you are taking up too much space." Everyone has at least one idea that can make them a millionaire. A creative idea always comes from a willingness to dream. A dream simply means that you think without boundaries.

3. *Resourcefulness.* Your ability to create something out of nothing, or to see what others cannot see, is what gives you an advantage. You should assess what you can do that no else is doing, and/or how you can make it better. This often takes time; so make the time to step back from your busy life, find a nice, quiet place and seriously think and dwell on what it is you want to create, how it's different from the rest, and what you, uniquely, bring to the table that *no one else does.* This is not wasted time; this is an investment in your future.

4. *Motivation.* Your idea (if it's a winner) should inspire action. It should move people in a persuasive manner. It may not happen right away, but it *will* happen—if the timing is right. Most important, it should move *you.* When I get motivated about something, it literally upends my daily schedule. I wake up earlier than usual, eager to get to it; I go to bed later than usual, unwilling to drift off to sleep until I get one more idea down on paper or one more e-mail off to my team. My clients are the same way; I can tell when they really connect with an idea and are on fire about something we've talked about or brainstormed just for them. This is what you should be feeling about your own ideas and, frankly, about your own potential.

5. *Destination.* Everyone enjoys a good road trip now and again, a meandering journey through uncharted territory that takes us nowhere fast. Ideas are different; they need a destination, otherwise

they are merely mental road trips signifying nothing. All ideas should have a specific, real, and definable purpose. They should have a reason or a meaning. There should be an objective or an intended outcome. Without a purpose, an idea remains an under-developed thought—liable to disappear as quickly as it appeared. Creativity requires that there be a destination in mind.

Knowledge is key and passion is powerful, but true imagination combines both information and inspiration. Women are naturally more creative than men. This is true: Women tend to see things in color, whereas men see things in black or white. The difference is in the details. Just look at how products are marketed to women versus how they are marketed to men. Chick flicks, for instance, appeal creatively to our sense of romance, fun, humor, passion, and whimsy. Guy flicks tend to appeal (mostly prehistorically) to men's fascination with guns, guts, violence, and pyrotechnics. The heroes may come and go, but the plot is essentially the same thing.

Women's magazines offer culture, criticism, fashion, quizzes, polls, and articles on a wide variety of creative and topical subjects. Men's magazines offer shiny pictures of cars, the latest techno-gadgets and varying degrees of bikini lengths. Men tend to see things in two dimensions; women need 3-D glasses for even the most basic things, particularly at work.

Cultivating your creativity gives you the edge. As I said before, if everyone is thinking alike, then someone is not thinking. Creativity is also ever-evolving; it's not static or fixed in place. Madonna has continually evolved over the years, not only displaying each new fashion craze before it became mainstream but, in many cases, creating it.

But clothes alone do not make the woman; Madonna has also revolutionized how music is performed, delivered to the masses, purchased, packaged, downloaded, and even simulcast across a variety of cutting-edge platforms. Her reward for such creativity? According to *The Wall Street Journal*, "Madonna just signed a gargantuan deal for herself with concert promoter Live Nation. She will receive $120 million for three albums and the right to use her name to sell merchandise."

Clearly, creativity is no longer a soft skill; it is a necessity for staying current, personal, and valuable to your organization. For new S.K.I.R.T.S., it is our greatest asset. The ability to bring fresh, new ideas presents a tremendous opportunity for professional growth. In a world of cookie-cutter employees, your creativity determines how you stand out; it is the "it" factor that makes people look, and think, twice about who you are, how valuable you are in the organization, and what you stand for, personally and professionally.

Walking through a department store, you see hundreds if not thousands of garments, handbags, shoes, and accessories. In a never-ending sea of merchandise, something has to stand out in order for you to decide to make a purchase. If it's a designer suit, maybe you like the fit or the color, if it's a pair of high heels, maybe you like the shape and the style, and if it's a handbag, maybe you like its size and convenience.

In any case, there has to be something unique about an item that draws you to it. It must catch your attention, or else it stays on the shelf. Once something sparks your interest, your next move is to look at the tag to see if the price is right. As women, we have personal tags, too. There is no price that truly reflects the depth of our worth and value. However, getting business and standing out in the business world *is* a competitive game. There is a never-ending sea of professionals looking to get ahead, get your business, and get your job. As a result, finding a creative, yet substantive, way to stand out is vital, not optional.

Remember, being successful is not based on what you have. Success is determined by *what you do with what you have.* Everyone has different T.A.G.S.: *T*alents, *A*bilities, *G*ifts, and *S*kills. Creating a personal recipe for a successful you requires that you use all of the ingredients at your disposal. This chapter is designed to help you personally identify your four unique creative T.A.G.S. by targeting the following.

Talents, Abilities, Gifts, and Skills (T.A.G.S.)

By personally defining what we have to offer, women discover we already have the secret ingredient to success: *creativity.*

Your spending power is essentially your ability to use what you have. Ability without application is like having a loaded checking account with no checks.

—Marshawn Evans

T.A.G.S. One: *Target Your Talents*

Everyone has unique talents that they, and they alone, bring to the boardroom. What are yours? Don't be concerned with whether your talents are specifically suited to your particular industry or even job; what unique talents you bring will only serve to enhance the job you currently do—or create a new job, product, or division entirely.

Many modern magnates lived very creative lives before they took over corporate flagships. Think of all the creative mold-breakers who now enjoy a life that is both creative and profitable, often beyond their wildest dreams.

Carly Fiorina, the CEO of Hewlett-Packard, was once a medieval history and philosophy major. Jimmy Buffett took his role as a self-confessed creative loafer and turned his beloved, fictional world of Margaritaville into a worldwide empire that now encompasses restaurants, theme parks, T-shirts, and more.

Oprah Winfrey's role as a reporter wasn't exactly your textbook MBA script, but today she helms a media empire most business titans would envy. And Michael Eisner, the future head of Disney enterprises, never took a single business course, securing two English degrees instead.

Looking at my own resume, it's clear even to me that I've built my own future on lateral moves versus that oh-so-linear, horizontal future espoused by advanced degree programs all across the country. And yet every so-called lateral move sent me leaps and bounds beyond the competition as I learned to grow into my creativity by recognizing my talents.

My frustration with the legal community taught me that knowing my weaknesses was truly a strength. You might be capable of doing something, but you might not be designed to do that thing as your calling. Competing as a Miss America finalist taught me that I could be an effective communicator (even in a swimsuit . . . remember, body language!). Taking a few months off from my career track to compete on *The Apprentice* paid off in untold ways as I used the downtime to network with some of the country's top players, male *and* female. In fact, competing on the all-female team was just the impetus I needed to write this very book, all about utilizing our strengths as women and sisters to advance our own careers through sisterhood and networking.

Action Plan for Targeting Your Talents.   Embrace your creativity; recognize your talents. Be unconventional, be personal, be unique, and, above all, be yourself. Recognize what you have to offer and don't be afraid to offer it. I meet so many women as I speak at conferences all around the country, and they always tell me how they wish they could show their creative side in more ways. Show it! What are you waiting for? An invitation? Forget waiting by the mailbox: Be a "Creativity Crasher" and show off your talents even before you get invited to do so.

This handy Action Plan for Targeting Your Talents will help you do just that.

- ◆ *What is it that you do, uniquely?* Ask yourself what it is that *you* do that no one else does—or that you do even better than anybody else does. Don't worry if what you do comes complete with fancy pedigrees or is "good enough" for your current job description. Linda Cobb owned a cleaning business specializing in disaster restoration when she began offering cleaning tips to her local newspaper in Michigan. From these humble beginnings, "The Queen of Clean" went on to found her own media empire, penning nearly a dozen bestselling books and appearing everywhere, from *Oprah* to *The View* to *Live with Regis & Kelly*. Linda did more than simply brand herself; she recognized what it was she did, uniquely, and did it to the best of her ability. That, in a nutshell, is creativity at its finest.
- ◆ *What is it that you and you alone bring to the boardroom?* Assess your company's vital statistics and find the niche you perfectly fill. Don't be afraid to defy convention, and be honest about what it is you truly excel at; fear is the opposite of creativity. Maybe you bake the meanest cobbler this side of the Mason-Dixon Line. Think

that's not a valuable enough skill? Think again. What if, to counter-act your company's low customer service ratings, you started having "Cobbler Thursdays" where you bring in a big-enough batch of your cobber for the entire customer service department to share, all as a pretext to get them fired up about giving the best service possible. Think about how that one day a week could brand you, not only within one particular department of your company but within the entire company itself.

♦ *Thinking outside the box.* Yes, you should definitely think outside the box, but be aware that the box is continually growing, or shrinking, depending on the amount of creativity in the company itself. No matter what you do, uniquely, it has value; from cleaning solutions to cobbler-baking. *What you do has value*—but only if you share it. You just have to find ways to share it, valuably, in a way that contributes to your own personal brand. Sometimes that takes ingenuity.

♦ *Creating the box to think outside of.* Occasionally, you'll have to create the box to think outside of! But that's okay; it's what creative people do. Creating the box to think outside of goes thinking-outside-the-box one better by starting something new— Cobbler Thursdays or Go Green Fridays—when adding to some-thing old simply won't do anymore. Speaking of boxes, have you ordered a pizza from Domino's lately? If so, you'll realize that not only can you do it online, but you can literally track the order from the minute you hit "send" to the moment it arrives at your door. (I've actually done this myself and, I have to admit, there's something slightly Orwellian about sitting at your laptop reading the words "Our delivery driver, Justin, should be at your door" and, at that precise moment, hearing the doorbell ring!) Gone are the days of phoning it in and hoping you get your pizza on time. Now you can literally watch the pizza be assembled and have a point person to contact if something goes wrong. So, in that sense, Dominos didn't only think outside the box to make ordering their pizzas more timely, interesting, and unique for their customers; they literally created a new box to think outside of. Take that, Pizza Hut!

T.A.G.S. Two: *Assess Your Abilities*

You'll notice that Chapter 9 is called Creativity, not Imagination. That's because plenty of people have pure imagination, which is in and of itself a blessing to cherish and enjoy. But in business, imagination without action is merely a bad hire waiting for a pink slip. But imagination *with* action is creativity, and that's what we're shooting for here.

It is said that Walt Disney was a man blessed with a vivid imagination, but where would the world be if all Walt did all day was sit on the front porch imagining mice who could talk, elephants with giant ears, dogs who dated over plates of spaghetti, and dwarves who whistled while they worked? That's right; without action, Walt would have been just another daydreamer and generations of children would be robbed of his vivid imagination and the scores of movies, cartoons, books, characters, and theme parks he single-handedly created with his unique and visionary creativity.

To put imagination into action, we must focus on our abilities. Being a woman in the male-dominated field of sports marketing isn't easy, but for me it was a simple choice based on my unique set of internally felt and externally proven abilities. My deep passion for marketing combined with a childhood interest in sports and the know-how to put imagination into action created in me the personal evolution that is EDGE 3M. EDGE (of course it's an acronym) stands for Expect Dedication, Genius, and Excellence. We want our clients to expect the best ideas from our agency. They come to use for ideas, for us to put our T.A.G.S. to work.

Think about the driving passions that have been hiding inside you all of your life. Isn't it time you let them out? Maybe you have new ideas for ways to run your existing company. What are they and what can you do, personally, to put those ideas into action? Maybe what you've learned in your current company, combined with an intense desire to do something completely new, inspires you to start your own company. How will you do it, specifically? What are the steps you'll take to begin your evolution from imagination into action?

As you focus anew on your inner abilities, remember not to let the past define you. What you did last week doesn't necessarily have to dictate what you do today, tomorrow, next week, or even next year. Dig beyond your resume to explore abilities you've never shared with anyone before, or only those chosen few. Remember that we are all characters in an unfinished book.

Action Plan for Assessing Your Abilities.   Don't just think about what it is you know you can do; do it! I can't overemphasize enough the need for action here. Abilities are all but useless unless you employ them, actively and regularly, in your organization. Hence, my handy Action Plan for Assessing Your Abilities follows.

- ◆ *Pushing the envelope.* If creativity is something that doesn't come naturally to you, if you're just now sitting down to contemplate your many and varied abilities, you may have to push the envelope on your comfort zone and try something entirely new. This may mean speaking up at those weekly staff meetings or, for that matter, knocking on your supervisor's door to make that bold suggestion or volunteer for that position he or she has been looking to fill. It's okay if you're scared; we all are at some point. It's *not* okay if you let that fear stand in the way of what you were meant to do. As my mother often said to me growing up, "Ask; all they can say is 'no.' " And how right she was. What if you face your fears and ask your boss for a few moments of his time and he— gasp—shuts you down? That's okay; ask to reschedule at a more convenient time and no doubt he'll remember you twice as often just for making the effort. What if your supervisor takes your name for that new position and you still don't get it? That's okay; at least you made the effort, and now that you've faced that fear you'll be twice as likely to volunteer the next time—and the next. Remember, creativity does not come over us overnight; it seeps into our lives, bleeds over the edges, until we are surrounded by it. Sometimes, that takes time.
- ◆ *Focus on your strengths.* You have strengths. You know you do. I know you do. But does your boss? Do your coworkers, colleagues, clients, or investors? Right now, pick one of your strengths. That's right, just one, for now. For the entire next week I want you to focus on this strength to the exclusion of all others. If it's

tenacity, be as tenacious as you've ever been. If it's networking, network your little tush off. If it's paying attention to the details, make those details really sing. For the next week, do one thing and do it well; do it so well that you just can't wait to share it with the world.

◆ *Address your weaknesses.* Seesaws are the ultimate learning tool for strengths and weaknesses; as one side goes up, the other goes down. By that philosophy, as you focus on a strength, curtail a weakness. As you revel in your strength this week, make sure to identify at least one weakness. What is it that you don't do so well? Are you nervous around people? Or, on the other end of the spectrum, do you tend to socialize too much? As you focus on a strength, tone down a weakness. Picture one side of the seesaw (your strength) going up in stature, as you practice tenacity or networking or paying attention to details, and the other side going down (your weakness), as you try to resist socializing too much or letting fear rule your life.

◆ *Know that knowing your weaknesses is a strength.* Going to law school and getting hired by one of the South's most prestigious law firms is no easy feat, and deciding after a few years that law wasn't quite right for me might be considered, by some, to be something of a failure. But for me it was an epiphany; a moment of utter clarity where in realizing what I didn't want to do, I could finally focus on what I *did* want to do. Which, as it just so happens, is what I'm doing—and loving—right now, this very minute. This is how the weak get strong and the unhappy get happy. This is how knowing your weakness becomes a strength.

◆ *Don't be afraid to bring your abilities to the boardroom.* Now that you've had a week to focus on one strength, it's time to actively apply that strength. That's right; bring it to the boardroom. Maybe you've been focusing on the details all week and noticed a new way to save your company money. At the next staff meeting, don't sit on this little tidbit like you always do (because one of your weaknesses is being shy about speaking in public) but instead let the cat out of the bag and see what happens. Maybe it's not the critical moment that turns the company around, but it could just be the critical moment that turns your (creative) life around. Maybe it's the moment your supervisor looks at you as more than just a worker bee. Maybe it's the moment your coworkers finally give you that long overdue sense of respect. Maybe it's the time your boss finally remembers your name. And isn't that worth raising your hand?

T.A.G.S. THREE: *GATHER YOUR GIFTS*

At first blush it might seem that the terms *abilities* and *gifts* are redundant, but look closely and you'll see that gifts encompass not only what you can do (abilities) but also who you are, as an individual comprised of decades' of life experiences, the people you've met, mentors you've studied under, books you've read, and places you've traveled. Abilities are what we can *do*; gifts determine who we can *be*.

For instance, the pop phenomenon and businesswoman that is Madonna has certain abilities that include dancing and singing, no doubt, but so do many other would-be music magnates. What separates Madonna from her rivals are the passionate and personal gifts she and she alone possesses, which include a creative desire to continually reinvent herself; the skills of personal branding; the wisdom to surround herself with talented producers, musicians, and fellow artists; and the cunning instinct she displays for media manipulation.

All of these gifts serve her well and each is unique to her situation. So what gifts do you have that not only contribute to your creativity but also elaborate on or enhance your specific abilities? If you can't answer yet, don't worry: By the end of this section you will be surprised by just how many gifts you possess.

Action Plan for Gathering Your Gifts. Remember that gifts are both divinely given and supremely earned. What do I mean by that? Well, take Madonna; no doubt she was a gifted and natural singer, dancer, and self-promoter growing up, but was that enough? Hardly. Today's competitive edge demands that even the most creative must remain on the cutting edge if they want to retain their creativity in the face of overwhelming and constant competition. So in addition to her divine gifts of song and dance, Madonna had to continually learn, adapt, grow, observe, listen, and earn those gifts that made her stand out for the ages.

So it must be for you. Don't just observe your gifts and pat yourself on the back. Use this Action Plan for Gathering Your Gifts to put them in motion.

♦ *Be unique.* Take time to celebrate your unique self. So many of us work eternally at blending in, wearing the same clothes in the same styles by the same designers. Would a little dash of color or some funky eyeglass frames hurt our image *that* much? Don't be afraid to let more and more of your uniqueness slip out from time to time. Maybe at first it's just cracking a joke with the girls at lunch. Maybe next it's speaking up at the weekly staff meeting. Maybe later it will be something more assertive, like asking for a raise or promotion, but you'll never know if you don't take those first few steps.

♦ *Take stock of all you've known and seen.* Part of being unique is adding up all the individual experiences you've had, the words and images you've seen, and the thoughts you've formed to determine who, exactly, you are and what, exactly, you have to offer. Don't think that just because you didn't finish first in your class it doesn't mean that you didn't learn twice as much as the next person. We have got to stop being so intimidated by everybody else that it gets in the way of being ourselves. Be proud of who you are, and cherish your unique experiences. They make you who you are and, if you let them, allow you to be so much more.

♦ *Rely on your personal network of mentors, colleagues, and passionate advisors.* What makes us unique does not always come just from inside. Who we know, the mentors we select to guide our professional paths, the pastors we see every Sunday on our spiritual journey, the trusted friends and associates we choose to spend our time with—all of these people aren't just gifts in themselves, but create in us gifts unto themselves. Let them work through you as you begin to more actively gather your gifts; let that be their ultimate gift to you.

T.A.G.S. Four: *Strengthen Your Skills*

By now we know what gifts, skills, and unique abilities you possess; what we want to do with T.A.G.S. 4 is to strengthen those skills so that you can master the art of creativity. We want you to stop treating creative outbursts like a holiday, birthday, or other annual event, and start treating them more like an everyday occurrence.

Amazon.com is one of my favorite examples of a company that is continually strengthening its many considerable skills. (And not just because I love books so much!) It is a rare day indeed when I don't visit Amazon.com to find some new innovation or unique way of finding a product.

Be it a "Listmania" user recommendation, author blog, or some cutting-edge manner of alerting me to a product I've shown interest in during past searches, I am continually amazed by Amazon.com's attention to detail and obvious investment in breaking new ground by enhancing its already considerable skills in online e-tailing.

Ask yourself what you can do today to strengthen your already considerable skills. Can you be more proactive about sharing them with others? Can you be more vocal in trying something new? Can you finally get those thoughts out of your head or off your diary pages and out into the world, where you can actually share them with other people?

In the words of my father, "You'll never know until you try."

Action Plan for Strengthening Your Skills.   Know that you already possess a powerful skills-set; know also that possession is not enough and that mastery of those skills is what you need to truly let your creativity roar! The S.K.I.R.T.S. in the Boardroom: Set No Limits Summit helps you to do just that. Furthermore, my Action Plan for Strengthening Your Skills will really help you rattle that cage and finally let your creativity out into the world, where it belongs:

◆ *Finding your skill set.* Saying "I've got skills" just isn't enough— even if it *is* true. You've got to identify those skills and, more specifically, find your "skill set" to see how those skills work together. For instance, if you identify "being a strong presenter" and "paying attention to details" as two of your known skills (see worksheet below for specifics), you can combine those two skills to unleash a powerful skill set on your next presentation. Think of how valuable those two skills are in unison; find skills you have that complement each other. For instance, people who work for or with me know fairly early on that I am a real "detail queen," and that if something isn't just right the first time, they're going to hear about it right away. People also know that I work quickly; if I say a report is going to be done at noon tomorrow, people usually find the attachment sitting in their in-box when they get to work the next morning. Now, both "paying attention to details" and "working quickly" play into each other because not only when you work quickly do you have to stay on top of the details to avoid mistakes, but when you make it a habit to read and re-read your work consistently, you not only make fewer mistakes but—that's right—you also work quickly.

◆ *Working on one skill per week.* To identify your skill set, pull it apart week by week. For instance, spend this week identifying and then practicing one skill. Let's say this week you discover that you're a really good team leader. How can you practice that? Lead something! If you're not doing something collaborative at work this week, don't worry. Volunteer to lead a Spin class at gym, schedule a book club meeting where you set the agenda and even select the book of your choice, or simply organize a family outing where you think of everything and then implement it. Once your week is up and you've mastered one skill, set your sights on the next skill to perfect. This is how you go about creating skill sets.

◆ *Combining skills.* All skills work just fine on their own, but some skills are actually more beneficial to you and your company when combined. For instance, as you identify and practice a skill each week, be on the lookout for skills that work together, like "team leader" and "plays well with others." Do you see how these skills might work well together? How about my skill set of "paying attention to details" and "working quickly"? There truly is strength in numbers, particularly when you multiply your strengths by two!

◆ *Applying skills to daily situations.* Skills in your head are great, but they don't really count until they come to life on the street, at your desk or particularly in the boardroom. So get in the habit of putting your skills to work by applying them to daily situations. Case in point: if "coming up with new ideas" is one of your strongest skills, how can you put that to work in daily situations? Well, you can add an index card with a new idea on it to the staff "suggestion box" every day. You can speak up in daily staff meetings, respond to internal memos or even craft memos of your own to the Creative Department. You can think of new ways to save time at the grocery store, new ways to save money for retirement, or even new ways to organize your closet to be more efficient. Pick a skill and start applying it to your daily life, and in no time you will have built something even more valuable: a habit!

Lessons for M.E. (Motivation and Empowerment)

In the final analysis, few job skills are as valuable as creativity. More than ever, imagination, ideas, and ingenuity are driving American productivity as they never have before. More people than ever before are working from home, working remotely, creating flexible work schedules, and starting new businesses of their own. Technology is a tool designed by the highly creative to assist in creativity. Let us embrace both technology and creativity to lead better, healthier, smarter, more productive, and more professional lives.

Jack Welch, the legendary retired CEO of General Electric, once said, "We know where most of the creativity, the innovation, the stuff that drives productivity lies—in the minds of those closest to the work." No one knows *when* you work, *why* you work, and *how well* you work better than you yourself do. Tap into that knowledge and recognize the unique and individual value of your own T.A.G.S.

In this chapter, particularly, I try to show you just how creative you can be. Remember, creativity isn't always butterflies and rainbows. Great ideas move great companies, and are often created by single employees. A new way to work, a new way to save money at work, to create a greener company, a more efficient company, a more profitable company—these are all aspects of a creative mind.

More important, being creative will help brand you at work. Many of us go through the motions, beating the clock and doing as much as we need to do merely to get by. Creative people know how to make every day count, because every day someone is watching you, listening to you, regarding you, judging and evaluating you. Don't complain about being where you are because it's your lot in life; get somewhere better by creating the life you truly want to live.

That starts with you, right now, today.

Set No Limits Reflection

I said it before: Creativity is merely imagination until you add some action to the mix. Now that we've identified your T.A.G.S., let's publish them with this short worksheet that helps you organize and categorize your blessed creativity.

T.A.G.S. ONE: TARGET YOUR TALENTS

My *talents* are:

◆ _____

◆ _____

◆ _____

◆ _____

◆ _____

◆ _____

T.A.G.S. TWO: ASSESS YOUR ABILITIES

I possess the following *abilities*:

◆ _____

◆ _____

◆ _____

◆ _____

◆ _____

◆ _____

T.A.G.S. THREE: GATHER YOUR GIFTS

I have the following *gifts* to offer:

- _____
- _____
- _____
- _____
- _____
- _____

T.A.G.S. FOUR: STRENGTHEN YOUR SKILLS

These *skills* can be strengthened:

- _____
- _____
- _____
- _____
- _____
- _____

Chapter 8

Captivation

*Get Their Attention with
Your Own Personal Brand*

Cap•ti•va•tion (*n***) to influence and dominate by some
special charm, art, or trait and with an irresistible appeal.**

Say the name "Suze Orman" and you immediately know what you're in
for: tough, honest, plain talk about how to get your finances back in
order. Whether you're reading one of her bestselling books, watching
her on TV or listening to her on your drive-time radio hour, you know
what you're getting. You also know what you're *not* getting: you won't
get a fashion line, you won't get her latest single, you won't hear about
how she's taking acting lessons or going into rehab.

You'll also get something that's not only hard to define, but even
harder to come by these days: authenticity. Says Orman's literary agent,
Amanda Urban, about her decision to hire an unknown how-to author
when at that time she didn't represent how-to authors, let alone
unknown authors, "She had such an authentic voice, and that's because
she completely cares about what she is doing."

Orman's authenticity as a living, growing, thinking, evolving mega–
brand name dates back to her troubled childhood, when a speech
impediment forced her to become extremely insecure about not only
her physical ability to socialize but also her mental ability to succeed.

After years of struggling as a waitress on $400 a month, Suze decided
to open up her own restaurant—but couldn't drum up the $20,000 to

$30,000 she would need for seed money. Some of her regular customers heard of her dreams and passed around a hat—a very *big* hat: by the end of her shift they handed her checks totaling $50,000!

Suze didn't know anything about saving, let alone investing, such a huge sum. A customer advised her to put the money with Merrill-Lynch and let them do the heavy lifting. Suze did just that, but an unscrupulous broker lost all her money in less than a year. Heartbroken but determined, Suze realized she could do the professional brokers one better and got a job as a broker herself.

The rest is history; Suze didn't just beat the brokers at their own game, but she took them to court, literally. After realizing that brokers have a code of ethics—and that her broker had broken this—she successfully sued Merrill-Lynch and was able to pay her original investors back, even though her dream of opening a restaurant was now ancient history.

Today Suze Orman is the author of nearly a dozen bestselling books on personal finance and has helped millions more personal investors—most of them women—through her various television, radio, and live performances all over the country. The little girl who never thought she'd amount to anything succeeded in becoming what *Investor's Business Daily* calls "one of the most popular self-help financial advisers in America."

She is also one of the most popular personal brands on the market today. She is not alone; many modern, successful women today are also very modern, successful personal brands. From Oprah Winfrey to Martha Stewart, from Condoleezza Rice to Nancy Pelosi, from Madonna to Beyonce, women as brands is nothing new.

However, I realize the topic of branding yourself may be new to you. Well, hopefully for not much longer . . .

Be Captivating, Be Yourself, Be Your Brand

As S.K.I.R.T.S., new or old, it is important that we continue to daily define ourselves in the workplace, the boardroom, or even the corner office. Branding is all about identity; knowing yourself to be yourself. This is not merely to get attention for attention's sake, but instead to cement our presence in the organization and secure for ourselves a brighter, more prominent future.

Many women complain about being "passed over" for this or "overlooked" for that, but instead of complaining about what's happened in the past, I suggest you start actively branding yourself at work to avoid anything like that ever happening in the future.

After all, you may have a dozen or more admirable traits at your fingertips, but how will anyone ever notice them if you keep them all to yourself? Just as importantly, how can you actively benefit the organization if you passively resist tooting your own horn? Modesty is a valued asset in this blaring day of oversharing, but modesty for modesty's sake is like trying to win a knockout with one hand tied behind your back.

At the S.K.I.R.T.S. in the Boardroom: Set No Limits Summit I ask attendees, Why be quiet when you can be captivating instead? Our goal at the intensive is to make you *so* compelling that when you walk into a room you instantly command attention. That's what bold brands do.

Captivation is about building a personal brand. The objective is to help women see their value and uniqueness as a way to leverage career growth. I think it would be good to highlight some power women who have leveraged their personal brands to build an empire. I want to show women how little things can make a huge difference.

One of my talents is speaking; speaking is part of my own personal brand. So with my first company, Communication Counts!, I packaged my talent and sold it a professional service for high-end clients—essentially doing public speaking training and consulting. With ME Unlimited, I speak professionally. Speaking has become a key element of my brand.

Much as Suze Orman's background in overcoming a speech impediment and working her way through the brokerage ranks has allowed her to establish her own personal brand, my own background contributed not just to my familiarity with speaking but also in helping me to realize its value as a branding tool.

In law school, I had to learn not only to speak in front of people but to think on my feet, speak extemporaneously, and control my insecurities to focus on the legal question at hand. I mastered this craft as a lawyer, and found the dual experiences of learning to try cases and trying cases doubly valuable as a Miss America finalist, in which speaking during the interview competition was of vital importance. Naturally, flubbing an interview with Donald Trump himself is one's biggest fear. My experience in and passion for speaking publicly helped me to ace it, instead.

And now we come to you, your resume, your passion, your interests, and your own recipe for creating captivation on a personal and professional level. Suze Orman learned finance the hard way; I learned to love speaking. What is it that you do? What are you interested in? How can you combine your interests and special skills to create a personal brand all your own?

You've got questions; I've got answers.

Strike Up the Brand!

What would it be like to rank as one of the 100 most powerful women by *Forbes* magazine? To be so well regarded that one of the, if not *the*, most respected financial magazines of our times recognized you and 99 other women as "the most powerful" on the planet?

Well, I didn't make it this year, but maybe I can tell you, personally, I'll be there next year. One woman who can tell you is Greta Van Susteren, former attorney and current host of *On the Record with Greta Van Susteren*.

Greta has an exceptionally refined pedigree, including trying cases in federal appellate courts and state supreme courts and winning the American Bar Association's Presidential Award for Excellence in Journalism. She later merged flawlessly into the competitive world of TV journalism, covering a variety of news stories with a legal slant until she appeared on the country's popular radar during the O.J. Simpson trial.

Though the trial made celebrities of many—Johnny Cochran, Marcia Clark, Christopher Darden, and Mark Fuhrman, to name just a few—Van Susteren's cool, calm demeanor, sharp wit, insightful questions, wry observations, and commitment to excellent has since put her at the forefront of legal reporters. As such, her own personal brand is impeccable and remains intact, while those who came before her, often more famously, have since started flying well below the radar.

Suze and Greta have clearly mastered the captivation angle, but what about you? How can you begin branding yourself, today, and create for yourself an identity that others will not only instantly recognize, but suddenly respect? Have no fear; I answer your questions right now in the following.

- ◆ *What is a brand?* In the traditional sense, a brand is "a class of goods identified by name as the product of a single firm or manufacturer," but we are much more than the sum of our parts. You might recognize Nike, Gatorade, Xbox, McDonald's, and AMC as brand names, and you'd be right. But over time brands have evolved from mere visual representations—the Nike "swoosh," the golden arches, the lightning on a Gatorade bottle—to living, breathing things that are designed to create emotion upon recognition. You don't simply recognize the uniquely artistic "Starbucks lady" (it's technically a "twin-tailed siren") on the side of your coffee cup, you equate the Starbucks brand with designer coffee, the good things in life, that relaxing third place (besides home and work) where you go to unwind, socialize, revive, and luxuriate. This is the true power of brands.
- ◆ *What is a personal brand?* Personal brands evolved alongside men and women as they eventually came to symbolize the faces of their corporate entities. Some of the most famous personal brands include Martha Stewart and Oprah, who are both brand names unto themselves and CEOs in their own rights. If the power of the personal brand is strong enough (as it is with these two women), the person and the company become indistinguishable. But many professionals have started personally branding themselves to stand out from the intense competition in their chosen professions. Jim Cramer has branded himself into the "Mad Money" man to separate himself from dozens of imitators. Tucker Carlson has his bowtie to distinguish himself from several other televised political pundits, Raven Simone has her family-friendly audience, Dominick Dunne has his tortoise-shell frames and Ellen DeGeneres has her self-deprecating, Midwest charm. All of these are hallmarks of the personal brand; the daily effort put forth to

distinguish one author, celebrity, pundit, journalist, financial advisor, or expert from his or her crowded field of competitors.

◆ *What is not a brand?* This is not to say that the distinguished journalist and legal insider that is Dominick Dunne is merely a pair of glasses or that the immensely talented Raven Simone is just another Disney product. Remember, a brand is not a thing, a logo, a gimmick, or a prop. A brand is a living thing, a collective feeling or emotion created—albeit consciously—by an individual who wants to shape a more visible identity for herself. In no way, shape, or form am I telling you to start wearing a tiara to work or inject more colorful clothes into your wardrobe or start yelling and waving your arms wildly just for the sake of wearing tiaras, being colorful, or acting crazy. A brand is not mimicry or copyright infringement; a brand is unique to you, germane to your way of life and, above all, a visual, purposeful, and personal representation of who you are inside.

You Are Already Branded (For Better or Worse)

Don't believe me? Ask someone, preferably someone you know and trust and see, even work with, every day: your best work-buddy in the next cubicle, the trusted colleague in the next office, your girlfriend in accounting, your neighbor, roommate, best friend, sister, or mother. Go on, ask them, "What's my reputation?"

It's likely that you will get a variety of responses all pointing to the same personal brand. You may hear words like "demanding," "bossy," "perfectionist," or "challenging," but you don't need to have a master's degree in English to know that all these words are painting the same picture. Maybe the words you hear are "geek," "nerd," "straight," or "square," but they're all saying the same thing.

That's because the picture we put out to the world is built not on only one comment, action, outfit, or accomplishment. Your current brand— or reputation—is built on a series of comments, actions, outfits, or accomplishments. It's not what you do one day to create a personal brand; it's what you do every day.

All I'm trying to get you to do in this chapter is to do the right things every day to create the brand you want, rather than the one you've been given (often undeservedly so) while not even trying. We don't want your default brand; the one you've been building, effortlessly, ever since you got hired. We want your ideal brand.

But first, we have to know the difference.

My Current Brand

What is your current brand? If you feel comfortable, ask around and see. If not, look in the mirror—critically, objectively—and write down what you see. Better yet, write down what you feel when you look at yourself objectively, as someone else might when meeting you for the first time.

_____

_____

_____

_____

_____

Having a little trouble? Let's see what I can do to help. Let me share what happened when a colleague of mine—we'll call her "Breanna"— tried this very exercise at her workplace.

People used words like "indecisive" or "hesitant" to describe my management style. I got the feeling that I was coming off as vague in my instructions; that the direction I was giving both equals and underlings wasn't very clear. One coworker said I "vacillated" a lot.

My Ideal Brand

Now step back from the mirror or the confessional and think about what it is you'd like to portray. Listen, I'm all for describing myself with words like "demanding," "bossy," "perfectionist," or "challenging," but maybe you're not so comfortable with that. Maybe the words you *want* to hear are "geek," "nerd," "straight," or "square." The point here is not to think about who you could be if you could be somebody else, but what you want people to know about you when they see you.

_____

_____

_____

_____

_____

Now, let's see how "Breanna" took her current brand and created an ideal brand for herself.

I didn't like hearing that my co-workers thought I was indecisive or weak; that's not the image I'm looking to project at all. If I could use four words to describe my ideal self, they would be "decisive," "clear," "confident," and, finally, "fair." I would like to build my own personal ideal brand on these specific characteristics.

Four Steps to Brand-Building

Creating a personal brand is a conscious, active process. You don't just show up to work one day fully branded and ready to reap the benefits without putting in lots of time and effort along the way. It's a little like going blond; you don't just leave work on Tuesday a brunette and show up on Wednesday a blonde. You work with your stylist to gradually, subtly, lighten your hair until, eventually, your look is neither shocking nor sudden, only . . . natural.

That's a good word, *natural*; your personal brand should not only feel natural to you but also represent you, naturally. As people begin to notice you more and more, you want them nodding in agreement, not shaking their heads over the incongruity with which they are suddenly faced.

Creating captivation is no easy feat; it's a fine line between drawing attention to yourself for the right reasons versus the wrong reasons. Naturally, as S.K.I.R.T.S., we are interested in the right reasons.

For *that* reason, here are my four steps to brand-building.

1. *Define Your Brand.* The first rule is to build your brand around your talent. What is it you do that no one else can? What do you stand for that makes you unique? Think of a brand as nothing more than a visual representation of what's at your own personal core. Those values you hold most dear, the tenets you live by, your personal code of ethics—these are the building blocks of your own personal brand. It can help if you break your brand down into two or three words, for starters. For instance, when you hear the name *Suze Orman*, you think of words like "tough," "clear," and "fair." Oprah brings to mind words like "generous" and "compassionate." If you *had* to define your brand in four words or less, what would they be? This is a great way to start defining your own personal brand.

2. *Develop Your Brand.* You have to define your brand so that you can develop it, because if you build it without knowing what it is, deep down, you're going to end up traveling in circles rather than in a straight line. Look at how Breanna, from our earlier examples, took her "current brand" and, after getting over the sticker shock, used her coworker's comments to create an ideal brand for herself, based on the following four words: "decisive," "clear," "confident," and "fair." Now she can build on each of those words to develop her brand. How? Well, for starters, she can take one word at a time. Let's start with "decisive." Some of Breanna's coworkers called her indecisive. What can she do to counteract their opinion? Well, she can start by making a decision and sticking to it. If she says "yes," she must mean it; if she says "no," she must mean that. This is a valuable skill to have and one that's easy to demonstrate. Once Breanna has taken a few weeks to master her indecisiveness, she can move on to the next word: clear. And so on.

3. *Deliver Your Brand.* It's important to remember that your brand can't exist only inside your head; you can't just will it into existence because you think you're decisive, clear, fair, and so on; you have to actually *be* decisive, clear, and fair—in public, in private, and at work—for people to actually attribute those traits to you. That

brings us to our third step: *Deliver Your Brand*. In other words, make it real for others. A good way to picture this step is to imagine your brand as an article you've written, read, rewritten, reread, and then rewritten again: Suddenly you've fine-tuned it to the point of (near) perfection and are ready to share it with the world. How? You publish it; you make it public. So it is with delivering your brand; you've got to make sure people experience your decisiveness, your clarity, your fairness—whatever it is you're trying to become. The best way to do that is to live your brand, every single day.

4. *Defend Your Brand*. So far I have placed a lot of emphasis on what you do around other people. Well, in our lines of work, that's a necessary evil; Most of us are surrounded by people all day long, every day. In fact, these are the people who will let us know—consciously or unconsciously—whether our efforts at captivation are paying off. But the best way to know if your brand is really working is to get to the point where you can be your ideal self *even when you think nobody's watching*. It's called defending your brand, and it's what you eventually do on the subconscious level that counts. In the end, that's why branding yourself has to come from within, not without. You can't copy Suze Orman, Jim Cramer, Oprah, or Madonna; you have to brand the authentic you (that's why it's called branding *yourself*) and to do that, you have to be yourself—your best self.

Stay off the D-List:
The Four D's of Branding Mistakes

Once you master the four steps discussed earlier, it gets easier and easier to brand yourself. Unfortunately, it's always easiest to undo the good work you've done by making mistakes that either devalue or deconstruct the brand you've worked so hard to build. Have you ever watched someone shatter their brand right before your very eyes? Like I said, it's easy to do.

Kmart was one of the original brands in the field of discount retail stores. Long before Walmart came to rule the roost and Target showed the Walton family how to really get things done, that big red "K" meant value to an entire generation of thrifty Americans, myself and my family included.

For a while, Kmart was *the* discount store to beat; but rivals quickly surpassed, then eclipsed, the original discount mart to the point where I can't remember the last time I've passed a Kmart, let alone shopped in one. How does *the* original brand become *the* forgotten brand? How does a company with billion-dollar holdings go from the A-list to the D-list? Simple: They must have followed *The Four D's of Branding Mistakes*.

1. *Devaluing Your Brand.* We all have a tendency to take things for granted. A gorgeous sunset, a romantic dinner, the ability to walk, see, or hear. When we take things for granted, we devalue them; brands are no different. By not appreciating your talents, your worth, or your expertise, you devalue your brand and weaken it, bit-by-bit. Brands are things to be built, not broken. I remember watching Star Jones on Court TV and being impressed not only with the intelligence of what she was saying but also with the clarity of her brand: She was the tough, clever, witty, and not-afraid-to-be-sassy former attorney who had my respect at word one. Then her fame grew, but her brand never quite did. On *The View*, her opinions often got lost in the sea of talk show banter that the new and different format from her Court TV appearances demanded. Then came her weight gain and her wedding, and her personal life eclipsed her professional life, to the point where she eventually became tabloid fodder—and not much else. I'm waiting for a Star comeback, but until then, we can look to Star Jones as a good example of how devaluing your brand can do grave damage if you're not careful.

2. *Diluting Your Brand.* People have limited attention spans; it's human nature. That's why whittling your personal brand down to three or four words works so well; for you, for them. We can concentrate on what you do best if it's well within a limited range of expertise. So, for instance, if you're a good saleswoman who

can quickly read the client, walk in, and close the deal, you'll quickly become the "go to" girl for such duties. That's why labels are so frequently applied. Billy's the "tech guy," Sheila's the "sales girl," Ronald's the "think tank," and Gina's the "diplomat." These labels stick because we tend to specialize in one area to build our brands. But when you get to such a proficiency in one area that you think all domains are open to you, you can start to dilute your brand—and eventually kill it altogether. Doing too much outside of your area of expertise and/or going outside of your focus area tends to do just that; it's like adding water to a powerful cocktail. The more you add, the weaker and weaker the drink will become. Work responsibilities are the same: The more you add, the weaker and weaker *your brand* will become. Think of actresses who suddenly get popular and immediately want to cut an album, design a line of handbags, be half of a power couple, open a restaurant, and run for local office. What do we call them now? Actress, designer, singer, politician? I'm not saying you can't wear several hats at work; we are much more than merely the "tech gal," "sales pro," or "diplomat." However, keep a close eye on your brand, and the minute you feel it slipping away due to your extra duties, cut down on one or two and focus on the skills that got you those extra duties in the first place. Chances are, that's where your personal brand is strongest.

3. *Diffusing Your Brand.* When it comes to branding, less is more. Do one or two things, do them well, be known for them, and keep doing them: That's the key to successful personal branding and overall captivation. Oversaturation, overexposure, giving too much—these are all signs that your brand is becoming diffused. You can look to Hollywood for a great example of how to diffuse your brand, specifically in the way the studios are currently spewing out sequel after sequel, and remake after remake. In 2003, Disney's *Pirates of the Caribbean* took viewers by storm with its combination of wit, charm, special effects, retro-adventure escapism, and lush, tropical locales. Johnny Depp sizzled and swords clashed and pirates were hip once again. The movie broke box office records, saved summer, made millions, and went on to

spawn two popular, if disappointing, sequels. The same could be said for *The Matrix* series and other disappointments like the dwindling *Blade* franchise. Somewhere between the original movie that made the brand so popular, the studios, the actors, the egos, the money, and even the fans got in the way, diffusing these popular brands to the point where oversaturation actually meant fewer viewers.

4. *Destroying Your Brand.* There is devaluing, diluting, and diffusing your brand, and then there is out-and-out *destroying* your brand. Unfortunately, it's not that hard to do. Being a copycat, not staying true to the core of who you are and what sets you apart, selling out for that big promotion or stepping on others to get where you want to go—these are all quick brand destroyers. The death of a brand is often preceded by a gradual, or sometimes sudden, loss of credibility. Remember, if you don't define, develop, deliver, and defend your own personal brand, it's doomed to die. Kmart wasn't the only company to kill off its own successful brand. Other once-megapopular brands like Izod, Puma, *Mad* magazine, Atari, and others have either struggled to regain footing they lost in the 1980s or 1990s or died altogether. What separates an Izod from a Polo, a Puma from a Nike, an Atari from an Xbox? In a word, the successful brand stays current, always evolving, ever-changing, feeding on what's new, and keeping abreast by staying in shape. More specifically, the successful brand defines, develops, delivers, and defends itself.

Lessons for M.E. (Motivation and Empowerment)

Have you ever heard a film critic call the movie he's just reviewed "captivating"? Ever asked a man what drew him to his future wife, only to have him tell you he was "captivated" the first time he laid eyes on her?

I love the word *captivating*; it's at once so romantic and yet so equally practical. It's an alive word, a classic word, one that—like all successful brands—has stood the test of time. Words like "charming," "enchanting," "alluring," and even "fascinating" are all synonyms for captivation, but don't have quite the same charm as captivating.

And that, in a nutshell, is what personal branding is all about. You want people to be able to use three or four words to describe your personal brand, but you also want your own personal mystique to be such that those words only *begin* to describe you.

To be captivating is to defy description; it is to be the polar opposite of uniform, bland, generic, or cookie-cutter. It is to dig deep inside you, do hard work to identify what it is you're really passionate about, and convey that passion to the rest of the world—and particularly the rest of your workplace—by defining, developing, delivering, and defending your unique and passionate brand everywhere you go.

And, again, it's not captivating to be gimmicky or have a flash-in-the-pan brand. The skills I've shared with you here are habit-builders, specifically designed to instill in you a sense of purpose and discipline so that you can not only identify what it is you stand for but also learn how to share it with others every single day. I encourage you to attend the S.K.I.R.T.S. in the Boardroom: Set No Limits Summit, and to gather more valuable resources at www.skirtsintheboardroom.com.

Think of captivation as the courage to share your convictions with the world at large. That's all a brand is, at the end of the day once all the dust has settled and you've boiled it all down; the courage to not only say how you feel but also *show* how you feel by living the life you've always wanted.

Suze Orman's brand is so easy to identify, clarify, and pin down because she lives it, every single day. It's not fleeting or faddish; It's consistent, persistent, and published. Greta Van Susteren managed to rise above the "O.J. Curse" that hobbled so many of her contemporaries specifically because she lives and breathes the values that are her personal brand.

Oprah continues to inspire, consistently, year after year, while Martha Stewart remains stalwart in her conviction that we can all live "the good life." Gimmicks, tricks, fashions, and fads don't last this long; this is personal branding at its best.

And it's all available to you, if you'll just "Stay off the D-List" and learn my simple branding techniques.

Set No Limits Reflection

Brands live and die according to how actively you practice The Four D's of Brand Building. With this worksheet, you can better prepare to keep your brand alive by practicing a-D-a-day:

Define Your Brand

I recognize that it's important to define my brand before I can develop, deliver, or defend it. To that end, here are some thoughts on what I want my brand to say about me—the real me.

◆ _____

◆ _____

◆ _____

◆ _____

◆ _____

◆ _____

DEVELOP YOUR BRAND

Now that I know what my brand can be, I hope to develop my brand by doing the following.

◆ _____

◆ _____

◆ _____

◆ _____

◆ _____

◆ _____

DELIVER YOUR BRAND

I can do the following things today—and tomorrow and the next day—to deliver my brand to my coworkers, colleagues, and supervisors:

◆ _____

◆ _____

◆ _____

◆ _____

◆ _____

◆ _____

DEFEND YOUR BRAND

I realize that the best way to defend my brand is to truly live it, day in and day out. Here are things I can do every single day to defend my brand.

◆ _____

◆ _____

◆ _____

◆ _____

◆ _____

◆ _____

Part Three

Skirt or No Skirt

That Is the Question

Part Three focuses on two critical, defining facets that are vital to extraordinary, outside-the-box success for women today. The first is *command* (L.E.A.D.ership): Learning to effectively Listen, Educate, Act, and Discern is learning how to lead. The second is *clarity* (vision): Understanding and arriving at a desired destination is simply the process of fulfilling vision.

Chapter 9

Command

L.E.A.D.ership Is in Our DNA

Com.mand (v) to exercise authority or control.

Contrary to popular belief, women are born leaders. They are the pioneers of time management, organization, and direction. If a woman can raise a family, singlehandedly prepare a Thanksgiving dinner fit for a king, *and* run a household, she can run a corporation and still have time to get her nails done. As the great Margaret Thatcher once said, "If you want anything said, ask a man. If you want something done, ask a woman."

Cleopatra became Queen of Egypt at 18. Queen Elizabeth I led England to a time of great peace and prosperity. Pocahontas saved Captain John Smith's life. Sacagawea became both a guide and an interpreter for Lewis and Clark during their famous expedition to chart America. Harriet Beecher Stowe sold half-a-million copies of her novel *Uncle Tom's Cabin* and introduced a nation to the horrors of slavery.

Clara Barton founded the American Red Cross. Sandra Day O'Connor became the first woman to serve as associate justice on the U.S. Supreme Court. Madeleine Albright was the first woman to be appointed U.S. Secretary of State. To say nothing of the political and cultural strides being made daily by such famous female leaders as Secretary of State Condoleezza Rice and presidential candidate Hillary Clinton.

So take heart: Women have a long, strong legacy of leadership roles for the rest of us to emulate. Now it's up to us to carry the torch onward to a new generation of successful businesswomen. To accomplish that feat, Chapter 11 builds upon the previous principles outlined in the book, and shows women how to speak up, take a stand, and make a mark in three essential areas: *company, community* and *career.*

When it comes to women in positions of command or leadership, it's impossible to eliminate the emotional aspects of their job performance. In the past, women have been falsely accused of leading with their hearts, not their brains; real S.K.I.R.T.S. know it takes both to lead with a commanding presence.

In this chapter I also share practical insight on the founding principles of Emotional Intelligence (EQ)—the ability to perceive, assess, manage, and positively influence your own and other people's emotions in a productive manner. Unlike IQ, EQ means being able to separate the message from the messenger and understand individual triggering mechanisms to avoid reacting emotionally to a purely logical comment, statement, or decision.

You will also learn about the following leadership styles—aggressive, assertive, passive-aggressive, and passive. Naturally, I provide my own S.K.I.R.T.'s twist to these four leadership styles—labeling them the Red Skirt (aggressive), Pink Skirt (assertive), Orange Skirt (passive-aggressive), and Beige Skirt (passive)—and, at the end of the chapter, provide a handy quiz so S.K.I.R.T.S. can determine which leadership style fits for themselves.

Finally, the chapter will also highlight how to build trust, decision-making strategies, negotiation tips, and how to L.E.A.D. (Listen, Educate, Act, Discern) using my Leadership for Life™ Three-Step Process: Receive, Reflect, Respond.

> *If men can run the world, why can't they stop wearing*
> *neckties? How intelligent is it to start the day by tying a*
> *little noose around your neck?*
>
> —Linda Ellerbee

The 3 C's of Command:
Company, Community, and Career

There is leadership, and then there is command: Command is leadership with a purpose. Command is being in control—not of every situation, every time, but of yourself: your emotions, your reactions, your comments, your decisions, in every situation, every time.

This is what separates leaders from commanders; leaders think they need to control every aspect of their leadership role, be it the Nikkei Index, the price of wheat in Angola, the weather in Kentucky, or the flight delays at LAX. Commanders know to harness what they *can* control and allow some slack in the areas where certain things are out of their control.

Many women resist assuming leadership roles principally because they fear they lack the essence of command. But commanders know that, like courage, true leadership is feeling the fear and doing it anyway. Commanders don't fear looking out of control because they've learned to act, not react.

What's the difference?

A leader will delegate her marketing team to prepare 5,000 copies of the latest brochure for the upcoming Job Fair. She may use a rousing speech, bully tactics, or outright threats to get the job done on time. When it turns out that *all* 5,000 copies of the brochure have misspelled the CEO's name and will have to be redone, she *reacts* by blaming no less than three subordinates and burning her bridges with the marketing department by trying to get them to eat the bill.

In contrast, a commander will also delegate her marketing team to ready 5,000 copies of the latest brochure for the upcoming Job Fair. She will stress the importance of getting the job done right and on time, but instead of waiting for an inevitable error to creep into the project, she will *act* now by checking up on the brochures regularly: their progress, their delivery status, even their proof sheets.

If she doesn't have the time to read every single word of the brochure copy herself, she will make sure that someone she trusts (with an eye for detail) will read them for her. If a problem *does* occur and reprinting is the only option, she will make sure the resulting bill is split between her own department and the marketing department.

See how it doesn't take any more time to *act* than it does to *react?* And yet so much more is gained by fire prevention than by putting out brush fires every few days. Not only does the commander earn the respect of her own department—by delegating within and assigning additional responsibilities—but she is respected in other departments as well, by including marketing in the process and by sharing the responsibility rather than ordering it.

The bottom line when it comes to command is control: self-control. You plan for what you can and manage the rest. But knowing that things will almost always pop up to set your plan awry, you head upstream and act accordingly, troubleshooting problems before they become disasters and preventing fires before they spread all the way to the corner office.

Likewise, command isn't practiced only at work; true commanders spread their influence over three critical areas.

1. *Company.* Loyalty is a huge part of leadership, and can go a long way toward fostering respect from above and below. Company loyalty is at its lowest nationwide, meaning that those who are loyal are already a standout. Command at work can best be portrayed in your particular leadership style, but more importantly must accurately reflect your own unique personal style. We can't hide our personalities, nor should we be forced to. However, commanders know to accentuate those valuable assets of their personality and downplay the occasional weakness. Again, it comes down to control. We've all seen the various personality types that tend to undermine an otherwise strong leadership style: the boss as friend, the confidant, the backstabber, the gossip, the socialite in training, the square, or the flake. Learn from others' mistakes by choosing what your colleagues see. Remember that your workplace is not your home: you aren't getting paid so much to be yourself as to be your best self, that self that knows that others depend on you and that work is neither a playground nor a classroom. Come to work prepared, put in your time and then some, stay until you're no longer needed, and stay on top of your product and/or performance. These are the keys to command and, best of all, they are well within reach.

2. *Community*. True leadership doesn't end at 5 P.M. It extends far beyond the reaches of either company or career and affords you ample opportunity to learn—and teach—others. Too often we focus on ourselves to the exclusion of our community, and suffer as a consequence. Your community—be it local, city, state, or even just a neighborhood—plays a vital part in your leadership role. Just as your company can't be an island unto itself, neither can its employees. This is where you shop, spend, sleep, live, work, and play. Many of your neighbors are also your customers, and the more you can do to reach out to the community, the more you can do to give yourself a leg up on the competition. Attend local events, sit on boards, chair committees, and volunteer when time permits. Not only do these opportunities give back to the community that has given you so much, but they also provide venues for you to practice your command in a variety of settings. For my money, that makes it win-win!

3. *Career*. I learned early on in life to never take a job, but always have a career. The lesson has stood the test of time, for even through all of my varied accomplishments across a variety of platforms—lawyer, Miss America finalist, Apprentice, speaker, consultant, CEO—I have worked steadily in my career as a S.K.I.R.T. Every experience has been an asset and none of my moves have been lateral; they have all added more than one rung to my climb up the corporate ladder, a climb that continues to this day, with this very book. Too many of us take jobs to the detriment of our careers. Jobs that take us down, not up; backward, not forward. Worse yet, when we treat an occupation as a job, we immediately have the word "temporary" not only in the back of our heads but stamped across our foreheads: A lack of permanence quickly leads to a lack of performance. Know that whatever job you're doing now has career potential and treat it accordingly.

What's Your EQ? Understanding Emotional Intelligence

Emotional intelligence. It sounds like an oxymoron, doesn't it? Aren't emotion and intellect two very different things? Not anymore, at least according to Dr. Relly Nadler, author of *The Leader's Playbook: How to Apply Emotional Intelligence.*

Dr. Nadler defines emotional intelligence, or EQ, in his book, "Emotional Intelligence can be described as an ability or skill to understand and manage yourself and your emotions and understand and manage others and their emotions leading to star performance."

One could write a whole book on EQ alone, and many already have. For our purposes, however, the key words in the above definition all come down to learning how to "manage yourself and your emotions." This is no easy feat, particularly in the high-paced, highly-competitive, highly-charged world of the modern corporate battlefield.

Yet "emotional management" is a skill you must learn to truly grasp the art of command. Not to become a rigid automaton for the sake of the company or your career, but to realize that as healthy as emotions can be, when not under control they can also sabotage you when you least expect it.

Consider the following very common scenario: You are faced with an unreasonable deadline to complete an already-challenging project when word comes down from on high that the deadline has become doubly more unreasonable by upping the delivery date from next Monday to this Friday. Most people would become upset at this news, particularly because the reasons—as conveyed by the underling messenger—seem so arbitrary. Just as many people would "shoot the messenger," lashing out simply to give a release to their emotions and establish they're no pushover.

A true commander would assess the situation, realize quickly that no amount of shooting the messenger is going to change the actual message, take the message for what it is, assess it internally, sit down with a trusted team, and *deal with it.* In the final analysis, the difference between IQ and EQ is not only recognizing your emotions but controlling them as well.

Just as important as recognizing your emotions is dealing with the stimuli that create them. To counteract the powerful nature of our very human emotions, here are some proven strategies for keeping your emotions in check as you learn more about EQ and its implications in the boardroom:

◆ *Understand individual triggering mechanisms.* We all have triggers; it's simply human nature. Speaking for myself, I can't stand negativity. I am a positive person and choose to work with positive people, so when someone approaches me with a sour look on his or her face and uses a negative tone to express negative words such as "can't," "won't," or "never," I'm immediately on the defensive. But that's okay; I know my triggers so I can deal with them responsibly, maturely, and, while I feel emotion, I can deal with such triggers without getting emotional. Your goal should be to identify your triggers. What has "set you off" in the past and forced you to react emotionally before you could really control it? If it helps, list your top-five latest blowouts; next to each blowout, list the trigger. You may see some common themes, such as "tardiness," "irresponsibility," or "placing blame." When you know your triggers, you can handle them; when you handle them, you can handle your emotions.

◆ *Separate the message from the messenger.* Every day, leaders are faced with two paths to follow: control or chaos. I think we all know how it feels to be led into chaos, and I'm sure that, given the chance as leaders, we would never want anyone to follow us into that nightmare realm. Unfortunately, unchecked emotions in even the most well-intentioned leaders can lead the entire organization into chaos if the leader isn't careful. Most leaders do just fine when everything is going well; it's when plans get derailed, deadlines get missed, or something fails when our leadership skills are truly tested. Often we learn of this news in the form of a messenger; typically the messenger becomes the focus of our anger, derision, guilt, shame, defensiveness, or outright savagery. But even as we hear the bad news we have to start thinking to ourselves, "Is it this poor assistant's fault that Phillips deleted the spreadsheet? Is it her fault that corporate is upping the deadline? Did she send the nuts to Boise and the bolts to Memphis, when it should have been the other way around?" Hardly; She is just the messenger and no matter what you say or do to her, the message still won't change.

◆ *Choose your words carefully.* Always be on language patrol; and not only for foul language, either, but for derisive, bitter, cutting, derogatory, or inappropriate language as well. When we act out emotionally, we often lead without our tongues and follow with our brains. That's why managing your EQ is so vital: Controlling your emotions helps you censor yourself when what you really want to say could burn bridges, tarnish reputations, bruise egos, or end careers. Often what is said in haste results in waste: wasted emotion, wasted time apologizing, wasted time worrying about apologizing, wasted time making up for lost ground. Find a tactic that works to help you choose your words carefully in the face of overwhelming emotion. It could be as simple as literally counting to 10 or biting your tongue. One of my colleagues closes her eyes at the first signs of trouble and opens them when she's ready to speak. Another simply nods once to signal she's heard the information and doesn't speak again until she's processed it. Don't worry if someone has to wait an extra five or ten seconds for your response; I'd rather be tardy saying something smart than early saying something mean!

◆ *Apply the 5-Minute Rule.* The 5-Minute Rule insists that the world can shift in five quick minutes; that what you say or do can either turn the heat up or turn it down, depending. I remember once when I snapped at a very good assistant for a very minor problem: the copier jammed. But it wasn't just the copier jam that made me lose it, of course. It was the fact that I should have told her to have the copies ready hours ago, the fact that I really needed to impress the client who was waiting on these copies, the fact that traffic on the way into work that morning had been snarled, the fact that I hadn't eaten—you name it, I snapped at that girl for a laundry list of wrong reasons. Fortunately, the client didn't hear me; my assistant did. In five short minutes we fixed the jam, printed the proposals and contracts, bound them, brought them into the meeting—and had to wait another three minutes while the client finished a phone call he thanked us for letting him make. Five minutes, and everything was right back to normal; only it wasn't. I had permanently damaged the relationship with my assistant and never quite got it back. She said she understood; it was clear she didn't. My point here is, what if the client had heard, what if my boss had heard, what if the board of directors had heard—what if I had actually listened to the nasty words coming out of my mouth? And all for nothing. Even if the copies hadn't been printed on time, would the world have come to an end? Hardly. I could have faxed them over to his office later or emailed them to his computer. Frankly, if I'd been in control of my EQ at the time and not so intent on blaming my poor assistant, I could have thought with a clearer head and simply *printed* the contracts and proposal from my computer. And that is the true cost of letting your emotions get the better of you: Anger, fear, guilt, shame, and blame all get in the way of common sense. When you're emotional, you can't think straight; when you can't think straight, you lead crooked—which is to say, not at all!

All "Four" One: What Is Your Leadership Style?

Over the years, I have worked with, for, and even led a lot of different types of leaders. Popular theory holds that there are two, three, four, five, and even more distinct styles of leadership, but in my experience many of these types either don't belong in the same category or need their own, separate category.

For instance, is your boss "The Screamer," aggressive, passive-aggressive, weak, or codependent? Which category does he fall into? What about the noncommittal leader, or the Bully, the Wimp, the Absentee Leader, or the Genius? Some bullies are effective, and so are some wimps—so where do you draw the line?

Well, this is my book and I get to make up the categories of leaders based on my own personal experience, so I've whittled it down to four basic leadership styles, each corresponding to a primary color you and I are both familiar with. I thought this color-coding might be helpful. After all, if we can pick out what color lipstick to wear each morning, how hard can it be to choose a leadership style?

1. Red Skirt (The Aggressive Leader). The Red Skirt is *bold, precise,* and *declarative.* Much like the color from which their name is derived, Red Skirts take command in a bold and decisive manner.

They are often referred to as "born leaders" or, less vocally, simply deferred to when leadership decisions need to be made. Red Skirts can afford to be aggressive. They are confident with their leadership style, but even more confident in their decisions. Decisive to a fault, they can often border on stubbornness if they don't step back and admit defeat.

2. *Pink Skirt (The Assertive Leader).* The Pink Skirt is *cautious, fact-driven* and *fair.* Pink Skirts derive from Red Skirts their confidence and skill, but temper that with caution, research, and an almost obsessive need to "cover all the angles" when making a company- or even department-wide decision. The difference between aggressive (forceful) and assertive (self-respectful) is all in the delivery. Where Red Skirts can be antagonistic and insistent, Pink Skirts are merely forceful and firm. They get their way as often as Red Skirts, but get their way without stepping on so many toes. Pink is a good color for them because they exemplify the confident brashness of a vibrant red but also waver toward the white flag of surrender, making their color not quite so bold and their actions doubly cautious.

3. *Orange Skirt (The Passive-Aggressive Leader).* The Orange Skirt is *vibrant, brash,* and a *risk-taker.* Orange Skirts lack the confidence of Red Skirts and the cautiousness of Pink Skirts, and must be wary not to rush into decisions too soon. Orange Skirts can be quick to lead but even quicker to blame when their decisions go awry. Quite often their risks pay off; occasionally they don't, but without the fact-driven questions of a Pink Skirts to caution them, they are often at a loss to explain what works and what doesn't. They rely on instinct, not information, and while their leadership style is valued by some, it can be seen as a liability by others. They want to be aggressive but lack the confident, robust nature of Red Skirts, so they circumvent their outward aggression more passively, often doing deals on the sly and without much fanfare so that they can take the credit if things go right—but pass the buck if things go south.

4. *Beige Skirt (The Passive Leader).* The Beige Skirt is *vague, quiet,* and *uncertain.* Beige Skirts are the watered down version of all of

the other skirt leadership styles; they lack the confidence of Red Skirts, the caution of Pink Skirts, and the brashness of Orange Skirts. Instead, they constantly question themselves, a deep-seated fear sapping the color from their leadership style and the confidence from their leadership decisions. Beige Skirts can be an asset in times of peace and order, but can easily crumble when change is needed or boldness is required; they are passive in almost every way, leading by default—and often at fault.

You Are How You L.E.A.D.
(Listen, Educate, Act, and Discern)

Leadership isn't easy, but as Spiderman learned in his very first movie: *with great power comes great responsibility.* In the corporate world, there is no substitute for leadership—and no avoiding it. Even if you are the CEO of your own company, who do you think leads the leaders? Who supervises the supervisors and manages the managers?

Even if you work from home, you must lead an assorted group of support professionals in your quest to provide service to your clients. Sometimes you even have to lead your clients to what it is they really need. That is why establishing your own style of leadership is so important; you are always leading somebody.

In a typical day I lead my office staff to professional and personal success. From the internal workings of my own company to the inner sanctum of my conference room, where top sports players look to me for my expertise and advice, I must switch hats and play the leader there as well; leading them to a successful campaign, program, contract, or event. When I outsource work, such as putting on a big event, I still have to lead the caterer, florist, DJ, announcer, and servers to my client's desired expectations. In short, leading never ends; so the sooner you learn, the better.

And here, at last, are the true nuts and bolts of leadership:

◆ *Listen.* Leaders listen; it's just that simple. Not because I tell you to, but because it's smart to. True leaders know to surround themselves with good people, so when you do that, it pays to listen to those good people. Now, the difference between listening to and cowing to those good people is where true leaders are born. Listening is not the same as giving in; we listen so we can learn, collect, gather, assimilate, and, eventually, decide. But it *is* our decision; that's why we're leading!

♦ *Educate.* Knowledge isn't just power, it's a powerful tool in the hands of the right leader. To gain knowledge we need education; we need to educate ourselves, yes, but we also need to educate our teams, coworkers, colleagues, employees, and employers. Don't horde information for yourself; share it with your people and apply the above rule—listen—to how they interpret the information. Maybe today's educational moment is that new article in *Entrepreneur* magazine; maybe tomorrow's is a headline in the *Wall Street Journal* or the numbers from the latest ad campaign. Don't be an information snob; education comes in all shapes and sizes, and is valuable whether it is big or small. That magazine article could point to a new hiring trend that means a different direction for the human resources department; that statistic could determine where or how often you spend your advertising dollars. School doesn't end with your diploma or MBA; the smart leader stays learning because she knows you can never be *too* smart.

♦ *Act.* To lead is to act. No, not act like a leader, but act, literally; action is the leader's best asset. Regardless of how much she listens or how much she educates herself, *lead* is a verb; you must act on that listening and knowledge and use it to lead; otherwise, you might as well follow. What's so great about listening and learning, however, is that it actually informs how you'll act. Your people will tell you how to lead them, if only you'll listen.

♦ *Discern.* Leaders are discerning; they differentiate between what to do and what not to do, where to go and where not to go, what to say and what not to say. They weigh their options before rushing into a decision, knowing that haste makes waste. When I started EDGE 3M, I could have opened it up to a variety of professions: actors, beauty queens, producers, writers, artists—you name it, I've worked with them. But I weighed my options carefully, added up my strengths and divided them by my weaknesses, did a final "gut check," and knew that by narrowing my focus down to representing athletes, I could not only be more effective but a more effective leader. Don't try to lead everyone, all the time; don't try to just lead the winning team. Lead your way, the best way you know how, and make bottom line decisions with the best knowledge you have at hand. Don't be torn in a hundred different directions; choose wisely between two or three options. In all things, think "less is more."

My Leadership for Life™ Three-Step Process:
Receive, Reflect, Respond

Finally, if you want to be a leader in every aspect of your life, you will have to learn how to react with true command of your emotions. This means split-second decision-making and instant assessment of all incoming data; think of a good leader as a better data-processor, always on the alert for new information to take in, assess, and act on.

We talked earlier about the difference between acting and reacting: True leaders act so they don't have to react. How do they act? With forethought, based on information. In short, leaders act first so they won't have to react later. This means constantly being on the lookout for potential problems and nipping them in the bud before they blossom.

If you think leadership is an isolated event, think again; it's a daily, almost hourly event. You know how your computer regularly scans for spyware and other viruses? That's the leader's brain. You have to lead unconsciously, on instinct—but not on autopilot—to affect a commanding presence at work and elsewhere.

This means you need my Leadership for Life Three-Step Process.

1. *Receive.* Take in new information without judgment. Don't think of it as good news or bad news; just think of it as news. The more weight you give to a piece of information, the less objective you can be in providing a calm, cool, and rational solution.

2. *Reflect.* Once you've processed the information, reflect on it. What does it mean? What does it mean for you, for your department, for your boss, for your company? How can you do damage control in

a timely manner? What can you do to resolve the issue, when, and how? Make a plan; always make a plan before rushing in headfirst.

3. Respond. Once you have taken in the information (received) and processed it (reflected) it's time for part three: *respond.* Tell your team what's happened, what it means, and how you're going to address it. Publish your plan by announcing it. If the environment is such that discussion is warranted, participate fully and listen actively. If a more declarative approach is necessary, deliver the message and delegate various duties.

Lessons for M.E. (Motivation and Empowerment)

Very few words sound like what they mean: *Command* is one of them. To merely say the word is to instantly sound more commanding. Imagine what can happen when you actually command?

And that is my challenge to you: *L.E.A.D.* Don't say you can't do it because you haven't done it, don't say you can't do it because you don't have any positive role models, don't say you do it because you were just hired or are still in the secretarial pool. There are always opportunities to lead, wherever you are: as rookie or veteran, in the mail room or the conference room.

If you're not ready to make huge strides at work just yet, take a class in leadership, management, or even public speaking at your local university or community college. Volunteer to teach a class, lead a youth group at your church, lead a Thursday night book club tour through the world's greatest literature, or simply lead your family on a weekend outing (without getting in any fights).

Salespeople have a simple motto: A.B.C., or Always Be Closing.

I'd like to amend that just a smidge to A.B.C., or Always Be Commanding!

Make leadership a part of your daily life and soon it will become a natural part of your work life. This doesn't mean become overbearingly bossy or a know-it-all; it simply means that to become more comfortable in a leadership role at work, you should assume as many leadership roles outside of work as possible.

Once you get more comfortable being in charge, you can gradually begin to assert yourself at work. Ask for that promotion; speak up at weekly staff meetings; make suggestions, volunteer for committees, seminars, or workshops. If there are no committees, seminars, or workshops, volunteer to give one. Leadership is addictive; once you overcome your initial hesitation and try it once, successfully, you will see why I'm so excited about leadership.

Like all things, there are various levels of leadership. You don't start by being a commander right away; you gradually build up to it over time. That's why the sooner you start leading, the sooner you'll start commanding.

And the more commanding you'll be.

Set No Limits Reflection

Earlier we discussed the four styles of leadership: Red Skirt (Aggressive), Pink Skirt (Assertive), Orange Skirt (Passive-Aggressive), and Beige Skirt (Passive). Now I want to give you the opportunity to not only identify your leadership style a little more specifically, but hone that style until it's pitch-perfect. If the Skirt fits, wear it!

RED SKIRT (AGGRESSIVE)

Are you an aggressive leader? Do you make decisions quickly, with authority, and expect everyone to follow? Then you might be a Red Skirt. Below you have the opportunity to list several reasons why you might be a Red Skirt, as well as opportunities to list the reasons you're not.

I am a Red Skirt because of the following reasons.

◆ _____

◆ _____

◆ _____

◆ _____

◆ _____

◆ _____

I am *not* a Red Skirt because of the following reasons.

- ◆ _____
- ◆ _____
- ◆ _____
- ◆ _____
- ◆ _____
- ◆ _____

PINK SKIRT (ASSERTIVE)

Pink Skirts are assertive without being aggressive, making them fine leaders indeed. Are you pink? List the reasons why you may or may not be in the following worksheets.

I am a Pink Skirt because of the following reasons.

- ◆ _____
- ◆ _____
- ◆ _____
- ◆ _____
- ◆ _____
- ◆ _____

I am *not* a Pink Skirt because of the following reasons.

- ◆ _____
- ◆ _____
- ◆ _____
- ◆ _____
- ◆ _____
- ◆ _____

ORANGE SKIRT (PASSIVE-AGGRESSIVE)

Orange Skirts water down their leadership with sneaky tactics that border on the passive-aggressive. Knowing that you are this type of leader will help you become more aggressive and less passive, which is equally as important as knowing you're *not* an Orange Skirt. Fill in the lists below to decide for yourself:

I am an Orange Skirt because of the following reasons.

◆ _____

◆ _____

◆ _____

◆ _____

◆ _____

◆ _____

I am *not* an Orange Skirt because of the following reasons.

◆ _____

◆ _____

◆ _____

◆ _____

◆ _____

◆ _____

BEIGE SKIRT (PASSIVE)

Beige Skirts command the way they dress: to be heard, not seen—and even then, they find it hard to speak up! Could you be a Beige Skirt? Are you more passive than aggressive, and twice as passive-aggressive as you are assertive? Your leadership color could be Beige. Fill in the blanks below to find out for sure.

I am a Beige Skirt because of the following reasons.

- _____
- _____
- _____
- _____
- _____
- _____

I am *not* a Beige Skirt because of the following reasons.

- _____
- _____
- _____
- _____
- _____
- _____
- _____

Chapter 10

Clarity

Vision Will Take You Where No Man Has Gone Before

Clar•i•ty (*n*) free from obscurity and easy to understand.

How's this for a quick, metaphysical mind trip for you: Anything that is and everything that ever was or will be first began as an idea. Think about that. Someone had to think about high heels, lipstick, pantyhose, and credit cards before they ever came to be.

Your thoughts have intensely infinite power.

Don't be afraid of new ideas—of speaking the unspeakable and risking the envy, unease, or outright indignation of others. Charles Brower, author of *Fifty Years Below Zero: A Lifetime of Adventure in the Far North,* once said, "A new idea is delicate. It can be killed by a sneer or a yawn; it can be stabbed to death by a joke or worried to death by a frown on the right person's brow."

How true—and especially so for women. Having watched the Old Boys Club grow and prosper even as we out-excelled many of our male supervisors and CEOs, we are almost programmed not only to think before we speak, but to *over* think before we *under*speak.

When you dream, you become powerful. When you establish a vision and truly embrace it with clarity, you become unstoppable. The number-one cause of failure, and the number-one reason many women fail to maximize their potential—more so than low self-esteem or gender stereotypes—is a lack of vision. For women, it is our strongest asset. Our vision is literally tied to our destiny.

Without vision, there is no direction and no catalyst for growth. With vision, everything changes. We still face challenges, but we do so with courage because we can see the bigger picture. Because of vision, your outlook, your poise, and your approach helps you place disappointments in perspective.

You recognize that success is not a one-time, off-chance lottery win but a process, and disappointments along your path to success become not failures but learning opportunities. Vision is like the core at a nuclear reactor: All around that central core, power emanates. Its uses, highlights, and intensity may vary—it's used more at night than in the day, more at noon than at 4 A.M., more on the weekends than during the week—but the central core remains the same, emitting enough creative power for a multitude of dreams and accomplishments.

Change is a part of life, particularly for women. The trajectories of our careers are less like straight lines and more like pinballs rocketing off of various bumpers and levers that come in the form of weddings, divorces, childbirth, pregnancy, and dozens of other "feminine issues" that are our birthright. If we wish to persevere, then vision, clarity, and focus are our three biggest allies; only while keeping our eyes on the ultimate prize can we endure the many delays and fits and starts that are part and parcel of the lives of modern working women.

Our vision is intrinsically linked to who we are and what we can be. Ultimately, every personal choice you make, and every professional risk you take, is a reflection of your own intense, personal vision. In regard to your career, when you clearly see your vision, the business world sees you in a different light. Women with a clear sense of vision exude an amazing presence.

Reporters like Soledad O'Brien, Christiane Amanpour, and Ashley Banfield exude a clear and almost palpable sense of vision as they report the news in a sensitive, passionate, and intelligent manner. Actresses like Angela Bassett, Helen Mirren, and Meryl Streep positively radiate the clarity of their craft and what they bring to elevate each role they play.

Athletes like Danica Patrick, the Williams sisters, and Sheryl Swoopes defy gender roles by competing with passion, grace, precision, and prowess, both on and off the playing field. And whether you like her or loathe her, presidential candidate Hillary Clinton challenged age-old biases and broke powerful stereotypes in a campaign year that challenged America when it came to both race *and* sex in the White House.

These are women for whom vision is almost a genetic trait; women for whom clarity is a part and parcel of who they are, what they stand for, and where they are going—and where they are taking the rest of us. The fashions and fads may have changed, but for successful women vision is a constant.

As a fan, I've followed Soledad O'Brien's career from her early days on MNBC to her later promotion to NBC and finally to CNN, where she's blossomed. But even in the beginning you could look at Soledad and see that there was "something special" there; we call that clarity—and with it comes untold rewards.

What do people think about you upon first introduction? With clarity of vision, you don't even need to open your mouth to exude a calm, confident, and knowing presence. Without trying, you will automatically command attention and garner respect. Cosmetic pioneer Mary Kay Ash once stated, "If people see themselves as a person they can become, and act as if they are that person, soon they will not be acting."

Explore New Possibilities

Lisa Druxman had a clear vision of where she wanted to go in life: be fit and be smart. It saw her through her master's degree at San Diego State University, where she earned graduate honors in Psychology with an emphasis in Exercise Adherence and Weight Control.

She used her advanced degree to manage such high-end health clubs as The Golden Door and Rancho La Puerta. And, when becoming a mother created new challenges to her life's motto, she saw the apparent lack in "mommy fitness" in her neighborhood gyms as a plus and decided to be smart while being fit, creating a unique new business opportunity for herself in the process.

Lisa took a break from managing those high-end health clubs and instead began teaching a local class of a few dozen moms and moms-to-be how to stay fit while staying smart. Capitalizing on a new breed of strollers that made exercise for new moms easy, Lisa started a company called Stroller Strides and was suddenly in business for herself.

She did well locally, eventually combining word-of-mouth advertising with TV ads to open a second location. She added certified fitness instructors so she could focus on the Stroller Strides mission, which includes the tenant: "We will help moms achieve their ultimate potential, both physically and emotionally."

She only had local aspirations at first. Then one of her trainers had to move out of town and asked Lisa if she could try out the Stroller Strides model in her new hometown; it worked, and Lisa Druxman had her first official Stroller Strides franchise!

Along the way she created a weight management program called L.E.A.N. (*L*earn *E*ating *A*wareness and *N*utrition) and later published a book on the same subject titled *Lean Mommy: Bond with Your Baby and Get Fit with the Stroller Strides Program.*

The thing that impressed me so much about Lisa's story was the clarity of her mission, the lean target of her audience, and the dedication with which she pursued them. Both the Stroller Strides program and *Lean Mommy* book targeted her core audience: moms who want to stay in shape before, during, and after pregnancy. Every image on her web site, her book cover, the key words in her copy, and the entire feel of her organization is warm, nurturing, and sustaining to this demanding but growing audience.

As a business owner myself and as someone who personalizes business pitches for men and women in all kinds of sports, I can tell you that few ideas I've seen to date are as clear in focus and vision as Lisa's is, and her organization continues to grow and evolve along that original mission statement: "We will help moms achieve their ultimate potential, both physically and emotionally."

Vision Casting^{TM}

Lisa—and a host of other professionally powerful women—instinctively does something I call Vision Casting^{TM}; not only seeing your vision, but literally broadcasting it—live—out into the world to make it *real, definable* and, ultimately, *reachable*. Vision Casting happens when you begin to not only *see* the vision but actually *live* it in everything you do, dream and say. You can learn more about Vision Casting at www.skirtsintheboardroom.com.

As children, we often begin to form the vision that will eventually become our adult lives. The Biography Channel is full of home movies that Stephen Spielberg shot before he was a teenager. We've all seen the adorable shots of Tiger Woods, at age five or six, using a putter that was nearly as big as himself.

Some of us take longer to begin learning Vision Casting. Life gets in the way; after-school jobs take us away from modeling, singing, reading, writing, golfing, or filmmaking. Romances sidetrack us; monetary responsibility demands that we take that nine-to-five job right after school instead of going to a design or graduate or culinary or film school, as our vision demanded. Matrimonial and family duties put our hopes and dreams on the back-burner for years, and sometimes even for decades.

But our visions persist. Would Lisa Druxman have become successful even if she hadn't become a mom? Clearly, her impressive resume attests to the fact that she already was. Would she have begun Vision Casting and applying her educational, entrepreneurial, and physical skills to a brand new business of her own?

Maybe; maybe not.

Visions, like life itself, aren't static; they ebb and flow with the beauty and grace of our personal and professional lives. That is why it's so important to remain clear about your vision and, just as important, broadcast it to the world. Let your family know you want to make movies, let your spouse know you want to go to design school, let your parents know you want to play golf. Share your vision, and your passion, with the world around you and, with each passing day, the vision becomes more real.

We often talk about "manifesting our dreams," but what does that really mean? It means making your dreams a daily reality by bringing them out into the open, a little at a time, and actually injecting them into your life. Maybe you've always wanted to be a Top Chef but life, work, money, or family got in the way. What can you do to physically manifest your dreams?

Cook. Cook for your family, cook for your friends, cook for your coworkers and colleagues and mentors and employers. Invest in, devour, and use cookbooks; TiVo every hour of the Cooking Channel.

Participate in workshops, seminars, classes, and co-ops in your community. Eat and shop and devour new recipes with relish. The world is large but relationships are small; people notice and remember your special skills—but only if you share them. Sometimes that means Vision Casting to a smaller audience.

Rachel Ray is the archetypal modern businesswoman; smart, strong, energetic, ambitious, and deeply passionate about her unique and driving vision. Growing up in a tight-knit family that loved to spend time in the kitchen, she gravitated to food industry jobs in her adult years: at the candy counter at Macy's, famously, but also less romantic jobs managing pubs and restaurants in upstate New York. At the web site for *Every Day with Rachel Ray* she explains, "I was surrounded by all different styles of cooking and worked in the food service industry in just about every capacity you can imagine."

But in Vision Casting her dreams of one day being a full-time chef, Rachel Ray—just like the rest of us—had to pay her dues. This included not only days of toiling away behind the scenes, but years spent learning her craft—in front of and behind the camera.

Explains Rachel, "You have to be open-minded when those early opportunities present themselves. Take advantage of them, whether they're going to make you a lot of money or not. I did *30 Minute Meals* for five years on local television, and I earned nothing the first two years. Then I earned $50 a segment. I spent more than that on gas and groceries, but I really enjoyed making the show and I loved going to a viewer's house each week. I knew I enjoyed it, so I stuck with it even though it cost me."

Whether she was preparing her *30 Minute Meals* for an audience of five in a grocery store aisle, 5,000 on a local cable TV program, or 5,000,000 on national TV every day, Rachel Ray was Vision Casting—with a vengeance.

Don't Just "Seek" Clarity: Create it With My Six-Step "Dreaming with Deadlines" Plan

Seeking clarity; I often hear this phrase and, no matter how many times I hear it, it always baffles me. It's like when people say they need to "find time" to do this or that. You don't *find* time; *you* make it.

You don't *seek* clarity, you *create* it.

Clarity, like Creativity, tends to be viewed as a "soft skill" in most people's minds: "It's hard to measure on a spreadsheet, so where do we put it? Ah, let's just leave it off the books entirely." But clarity is the glue that holds many a company together through good times and bad.

Amazon.com originally launched itself as "the world's biggest bookstore," but when Amazon branched out from books into music and DVDs and then to just about anything else on the planet, many worried that they might lose sight of their original vision. But over the years, the clarity of founder Jeff Bezos's mission to "start with the customer and work backwards" has allowed the company to treat blenders and running shoes with the same respect and passion with which they treat Dickens, Angelou, and Bronte.

You don't have to be the nation's foremost authority on fitness for new mothers, the country's most easily recognized 30-minute chef, or the world's largest e-tailer to experience, manifest, and profit from vision in your own life. All you need to do is harness that vision and see it through the precise and focused lens of clarity. In the chapter on Creativity, I talked about the vast difference between being imaginative and being creative; the same holds true for clarity.

How many children shot home movies as a tyke or took up a sport when they were kids? Millions, I'm sure. Now, how many became Steven Spielberg or Tiger Woods, to say nothing of Tina Fey or the Williams sisters? Clarity is the bridge linking a strong vision with a strong purpose. I think of clarity as *precision*. When it comes to clarity, in other words, the focus is really *goal setting* and *dreaming with deadlines*; it's all about encouraging women to make a plan and execute it in a focused way— with proven parameters.

"Dreaming with deadlines" is more than just some cute phrase I cooked up to sell more books. It is a philosophy I've lived by, ever since I was a child and my many childhood schemes, inventions, businesses, or investments went by the wayside because I had so many I simply couldn't focus on one at any given time. But when I grew older and began defining my dreams by not only writing them down but giving them plans and parameters—dreaming with deadlines—that was when they finally started to come true.

These are the six steps I cover to help women "dream with deadlines" at the S.K.I.R.T.S. in the Boardroom: Set No Limits Summit. They are described in the following sections.

STEP ONE: CREATE A VISION

Visions just don't create themselves; they lurk in the back of our brains, vaguely informing us of their intentions but remaining perfectly content to loiter or gawk until we finally bring them out into the harsh light of day and force them to reveal their ulterior motives. That's right; you have to actively create a vision for it to become of value to you.

Visions tend to be elaborate; they feed mainly on pictures and images of us doing things we've only ever imagined. Sometimes we have visions of the success we've created, but not the hard work and effort we used to get there. It's a little like picturing a yacht out at sea without remembering to stock the fridge with caviar, or fill the engine with gas.

It helps if we filter the grandiosity of our visions into the reality of a real and identifiable single statement. I find "The One-Line Lesson" really helps us to focus—to an extreme—our vision with clarity. So let's warm up by using the lines below to roughly flesh out your vision. Take as much space as you need and brainstorm your vision.

_____

_____

_____

_____

_____

_____

Got it? Maybe you still need some help. Here is an example of a spitballing session where a colleague described her vision to start a new company designing dress shoes for women with bad feet.

Shoes need to be glamorous but comfortable; stylish but still healthy. Need to find distributor, designer—have someone help with finances. COMFORT IS KEY!!! Budget for prototype; understand trademark and copyright laws . . .

Okay, there is *way* too much information for a vision in that statement. It reads more like a business plan. But this is filtering down your dreams, ideas, fears, worries, frustrations, and hopes into a single statement you can repeat every day when you get up—and find focus with clarity.

So let's refine those ramblings into a more precise, three-sentence statement, and then go from there.

1. _____

2. _____

3. _____

Still scratching your head? Let's see how Ms. Shoe Designer did on her three-sentence statement.

1. *A comfortable line of shoes you'd be "comfortable" wearing to the Oscars.*
2. *Shoes for women who won't trade comfort for fashion.*
3. *Comfortable shoes that don't skimp on classy.*

Okay, we're starting to sound like ad executives here, but you get the idea. With each of the above statements, Ms. Shoe Designer is gaining clarity in her vision. What's the one word that stands out with all three bullet points? That's right: *comfort*. So comfort is quickly becoming the focus point of her vision. Now, let's work hard one last time to focus your driving vision into a single sentence you can feel comfortable with.

_____

_____

How did Ms. Shoe Designer do?

1. *I want to create a company that will design and manufacture shoes women can wear from work to a workout to a wedding!*

It's simple, really, but do you see how that vision could drive every motion Ms. Shoe Designer makes from here on in. That vision could drive the ad copy, the sales brochures, the materials she either uses in her shoes or rejects, the design—even the hiring of the designers, manufacturers, or promoters.

Remember, your vision should be based solely on your goals, not the expectations of others. You may need to get a few promotions on the way to your vision of becoming CEO, but no matter how hard you work for others, insist that you work twice as hard for yourself.

Finally, realize that this is not some futile exercise or busy work. Writing dreams down gives them tangible life—just like birth. Dreaming is the conception, passion is the pregnancy, and writing them down is the first sign that a birth is on the way.

STEP TWO: SET PURPOSE DRIVEN GOALS

How will you create your comfortable line of luxury shoes or your career in the culinary arts or professional sports? A vision is one thing; action gives that vision clarity. And how do we dole out action? In a *Rocky* movie; action is easy. In 90 seconds or less, Sylvester Stallone strips down, bulks up, learns some new technique, keeps it a secret, gets words of wisdom from ringside, and is ready to triumph over evil—all set to a rousing soundtrack designed to get your adrenaline pumping.

In real life, of course, life is not so easy. We need goals that we can achieve, accomplishments we can recognize, and benchmarks we can, well, benchmark—with or without the thumping soundtrack. All of this starts with one goal and continues to the next. Every goal should have a purpose; a goal without a purpose is like a tire without cars: it may look pretty, but it ain't going anywhere anytime soon!

To give goals purpose, we have to determine objectives. What is it we want to accomplish? More importantly, how? Just as importantly, when? Remember, these are dreams with deadlines; open-ended goals provide little value as compared with purpose-driven goals, which determine both a *what* and a *when*.

You must also consider short-term versus long-term goals; job goals versus career goals. For instance, for Ms. Shoe Designer, a *career goal* might be becoming the first comfortable shoe designer for women. How will she do that? By completing *job goals* in which she gains experience in all aspects of the footwear industry. Maybe she can work for a summer selling shoes at Foot Locker or Payless. Maybe she can move up to management in one such company to discover how decisions are really made; this will inform her shoe designs to incorporate real-life, real-time issues made at the management and sales levels to better ensure her success. Another job goal could be writing a blog on shoe design, getting feedback from commentators and advice from editors. She might even sacrifice time and money to intern for a shoe designer at some point; this might save her thousands later on, as she could now design her own shoes without hiring someone else to do it for her.

I admit, none of the above goals are easy; all are vital to Ms. Shoe Designer's success. See how each of her goals has a clear-cut purpose. For instance:

- *Purpose:* I want to learn to design my own shoes so I don't have to hire a designer.
- *Goal:* I want to intern for a shoe designer.
- *Purpose:* I want to know who my audience is when I actively start pitching my shoe designs to retail outlets.
- *Goal:* I will work the floor and then manage a real shoe store.
- *Purpose:* I want to know what real people think about today's top shoes.
- *Goal:* I'll start up a shoe design blog and actively read my site's commentors.

See how the purpose comes before the goal, and not the other way around? Yet in real life, we often flip that script and put the goals before the purpose—*if* our goals have any purpose at all. It's like a colleague of mine who starts a new diet every five or six weeks; she sets a goal of losing 40 pounds but, when pressed, always caves on the purpose.

Is the goal of losing weight to fit into a bikini for swimsuit season? Impress her new man? Buy a new dress? These purposes are fine, in the short term, but it's like having a career goal without being willing to make job goals; since her purposes are so fleeting, they don't provide enough motivation to achieve the ultimate goal, let alone the short-term goals.

We can also track Ms. Shoe Designer's job goals:

◆ Sell shoes over the summer.
◆ Manage a retail shoe store.
◆ Intern with a top shoe designer.
◆ Write articles/a blog about shoe design.

These goals help us identify her career goal:

◆ I want to one day run my own shoe design company and will work through various job goals to achieve that ultimate career goal.

STEP THREE: DETERMINE NECESSARY RESOURCES

To bring your vision to life, you cannot live on an island. (Unless, of course, your vision is to eat nothing but coconuts for the rest of your life!) Vision is the thing that grows inside us before we release it onto the world with Vision Casting. Every product you hope to sell, movie you want to make, competition you want to win, widget you hope to create, or song you hope to sing needs not only an audience to purchase it but also a "team" of not just people but other resources to help you create it.

Think Ms. Shoe Designer can design shoes on her own? Well, design them, yes; anyone with a pad and a pencil can design shoes, dresses, buildings, storyboards, or whatever. But what about when she's ready to put those designs to the test and wants to actually produce a pair of shoes—let alone enough shoes to stock a single Foot Locker or Payless retail outlet? She's going to need fabric and other materials for the shoes themselves, a factory for production and production workers to assemble the shoes, a promoter and sales team to help her sell the shoes, and a delivery system to get them where they need to go on time.

What about a 1-800 number to field complaints? A credit card company to take large orders or a bank to give her a loan to expand? Who will schedule her interviews with *Inc.* magazine and *Entrepreneur*? How will she find time to write a book about her experiences to help her inspire others? All of these things exist far afield of a vacuum. Here are the major resources you will need to help your vision come to life:

◆ *People:* Who can help you Vision Cast? Does someone in your family work in the field where you want to excel? Can you talk to a mentor who's done what you want to do? Not only that, but who will physically facilitate your vision, such as the factory workers to staff your plant or the commercial real estate broker you'll need to find warehouse space?

◆ *Places:* Will your job require travel? A new warehouse? An *old* warehouse? Can you work from home? From abroad?

◆ *Education:* What special skills or training will you need to achieve your goals? Will one or two computer classes cover it or will you need an advanced degree?

◆ *Training:* Do you have the time to get a real-life education in cooking like Rachel Ray or can you afford to go to a culinary school and become a classically trained chef like Julia Childs?

◆ *Mentors:* Who can help you along the way? Is your boss willing to be a mentor? What about your supervisor? How about your professors, classmates, friends, or family?

◆ *Information:* Information is key to bringing clarity to your vision. After all, imagining things one way and then experiencing them for yourself are two different things. Where will you get your information? Is it available on the Internet? Can you get it from real life or do you need to find it in a classroom?

◆ *Et cetera:* What else will you need?

Step Four: Assign Tasks

Tasks are the cement that binds your vision to reality. It's easy to get caught up in hearing the crowd cheer your name or rehearsing your acceptance speech for Best Business Woman Ever; it's much harder to get caught up in the day-to-day details of how, exactly, you will achieve that honor or win that award in the first place.

Tasks are the answer. Unfortunately, since this is your vision, you are naturally the one responsible for assigning (yourself) the tasks. You can't blame a boss for not assigning the right task or a coworker for not completing the task; this is self-directed behavior and it begins—and ends—with you.

Don't fret; I've got another handy acronym to help you assign your very first T.A.S.K.

- *"T" stands for Today:* Your tasks must live in the present; they can't be ancient history or the relative science fiction of tomorrow. You can't say "my first task . . . starts tomorrow" or "my task to lose weight . . . starts Monday." Tasks are not far-ranging goals or career aspirations; tasks are the actual, physical things you do *every day* to achieve your goals and have a career in the first place.
- *"A" stands for Activity:* Your tasks must be active, physical, challenging, and useful. "Drive to the community college and get a catalog of summer classes" is a great task, but *only* if you actually sign up for one of the classes. Likewise, "Sign up for that computer class at the community college" is a great task *if* you complete the day-to-day tasks that the course requires for graduation.
- *"S" stands for Serious:* as in serious business. This is not my version of a to-do list you tack on your fridge and forget about until it's time for spring cleaning again; these tasks *are* serious business. Each task you set for yourself builds upon the foundation of your vision, but foundations are meaningless if they don't constitute the bedrock of a larger and more meaningful accomplishment. After all, what is a floor without a roof? And what is a roof without four walls to hold it up and keep the elements out?
- *"K" stands for Kinetic:* as in kinetic energy or motion. You must keep your tasks positively moving in order for them to be effective. Let's say you set yourself the task of writing an article for an industry newsletter. This task will not only help you polish your writing skills but it will also make you stand out at work and accomplish your longer-range goal of getting that new position in the PR Department more quickly. But what happens if you start the process only to abandon it because time got in the way, work got in the way, family got in the way, or health got in the way? These are all stoppages of motion; you must keep moving with kinetic energy if you are to ultimately complete your task of completing the article. Otherwise, you might as well have not committed to writing the article in the first place as all those goals you wanted for

yourself—positive recognition at work and a possible position in PR—will become just more tasks you didn't complete.

STEP FIVE: *SET A TIMELINE*

Dreaming with deadlines only works if you actually have deadlines to work against. And not just deadlines in place, but deadlines in place with penalties—and rewards—for meeting your benchmarks.

For instance, let's say part of your vision is spreading the word around the country of your idea, experience, expertise, or story. You want to give seminars and participate in workshops and keynote conferences for a good portion of the next few years, building your name, meeting people, and completing this specific part of your vision. The only catch is, it's time- and cost-prohibitive to research, locate, and contact every single conference, seminar, and workshop all over the country.

So you decide to join a speaker's bureau and let these professional people do all that work for you. One more hiccup: The speaker's bureau only wants you if you have a book published on the topic of your speech! Wow, this *is* a hurdle, but it's a hurdle you can at least identify and, if you get right to work, rectify.

This is a dream with a deadline.

Let's say you find out this information in August and you want to start speaking the following June. The speaker's bureau knows a publisher who will look at your manuscript and get it out in a rush order in six months—but only if you give them the manuscript by January 1. Yes, a deadline; a real deadline. So now you can set to work on realizing this dream by giving it a deadline.

So you set up a schedule for yourself.

♦ *August:* Research, outline, plan, and commit to writing the Table of Contents of your nine-chapter book.
♦ *September:* Write the first three chapters.
♦ *October:* Write the middle three chapters.
♦ *November:* Write the final three chapters.
♦ *December:* Read, edit, re-read, rewrite (if necessary) all nine chapters.
♦ *January 1:* Turn in final draft!

To help you focus on this timeline and keep yourself in check, it's important to punish yourself for getting off task and reward yourself for staying on target. For instance, if you skip one of your chapters in October that means you have to write four in November. You may think that's punishment enough, but it's not.

Think about why you missed the deadline of three chapters in October in the first place. Was it because you've been partying too hard, watching too much TV, going to see too many movies, or reading too many gossip blogs on the web? Well, if so, here is a great chance to punish yourself. Cut back on one night of partying per week, one hour of TV per night, one movie per week, or one hour of blog-reading per day.

Don't just nod and move on: Take that in and realize that these are real punishments you can impose on yourself. Why? Because not only will rectifying the behavior that caused you to miss your deadline in October free up more time to meet your deadline next month, but recognizing the fact that these items are, in fact, deadline killers will help you avoid them next time.

Then again, if you exceeded or just plain met your deadline of three chapters in October, absolutely, positively, and without guilt or reflection reward yourself. Take a day off from the book entirely and see five movies in a row, go shopping and buy a new dress, rent a room, and take a long weekend—with *no* laptop! It is important to reward ourselves, because rewards creative positive momentum in our progress.

In essence, the reward lives long after the movie is over, the dress gets faded, or the bill comes due for that long, luxurious weekend. We begin to associate completing deadlines with positive reinforcement—and the more often we do it the more often we are rewarded.

Step Six: *Follow-up and Assessment*

For our visions to become reality, it is important to re-assess our goals as times—and priorities—change. And it's important to do this continually throughout the process, not just in one fell swoop at the end. I know it's tempting to do a once-a-year check-in, but to be effective the follow-up and assessment needs to be (a lot) more active and regular than that.

For instance, as Ms. Shoe Designer goes about her "job goals" of working in retail or interning for a designer or blogging to reach her "career goals," it's important for her to assess every step of the process to make sure she's on task and learning all she needs to know along the way. How can she do this? Simple: as she starts each task, she can focus herself on a strategic goal with a readily identifiable deadline: I will learn all phases of the retail shoe storefront by the end of my summer job.

This gives her not only an attainable goal, but a verifiable timeline with which to assess her progress and measure the results. In the first week or two of her employment at Foot Locker or Payless, for instance, she might draw up a list of the "six main elements of the retail shoe process." This list may contain such items as "customer service," "inventory," "scheduling," and so on.

The more clearly you can identify the outcome you want to achieve, the easier it is to assess your performance. Maybe she's a natural people person and ticks "customer service" off fairly quickly. Perhaps Ms. Shoe Designer is a details person and never has a problem keeping the shelves stocked or the items in back in order.

However, maybe she finds it harder to make demands of others and/ or delegate, so that not only are her coworkers, employers, and even employees taking advantage of her, but she lets them off the hook too easily when they call in sick or ask for days off—making her lacking in the "scheduling" department. By assessing her performance in the beginning, middle, and end of her employment, she can follow-up with an active game plan to correct her behavior at regular intervals before it's too late.

Likewise, as you write your imaginary book for your imaginary speaking company, you can look at the timeline and build in periods for follow-up and assessment. For instance, each month has four weeks, but each month you only have to write three chapters. So you could schedule yourself for a chapter each week, and then use the last week of every month to follow-up to make sure you're meeting your deadlines, and also to assess if the writing is up to snuff for your publisher.

The important thing to remember about follow-up and assessment is that it's not just another soft skill; I didn't put it last because it's least important. I put it last because you have to actually *do something* to assess and follow-up with! We can all get in the habit of ticking off items on our to-do list without actually stopping to see if those items are (a) completed, (b) of quality, and (c) actively contributing to our sense of vision.

In fact, it's actually more important to assess and find yourself lacking so that you can go back and start over or correct yourself, than it is to simply accomplish things quickly at the expense of your ultimate goal.

For instance, it does Ms. Shoe Designer no good to go to the trouble of working an entire summer at a retail shoe store if she doesn't excel at her job and conquer the onerous duty of scheduling her staff properly just as it does you—or your publisher—no good to turn in a project that's essentially "sloppy copy."

Like my father Carter Evans always said, "A job worth doing is worth doing well."

Follow-up and assessment separates the mere jobs from jobs done well.

> *"Vision is like adrenaline. It makes you do what you never thought you could."*
> —Marshawn Evans

Lessons for M.E. (Motivation and Empowerment)

We all know people who lack clarity. They start ambitious projects only to abandon them when the materials aren't readily available, the directions get too complicated, the commute gets too far away, the practice gets too time-consuming, or the cost gets too high.

They have closets full of sports gear they've only used once, bookshelves lined with textbooks from courses they never finished or self-help books they never read, and garages or basements chockful of fancy exercise equipment they now use as expensive clothes hangers.

Clarity is the great equalizer; it doesn't require advanced degrees, beauty, extreme talent, or even money. We can all have clarity—all it takes is time and a little effort—and it not only sets us apart at work but sets us moving down the path toward goals accomplished, tasks met, and dreams achieved.

In this chapter I have given you countless tools to help you have more clarity at work, at home, and in life in general. They will be worth nothing if your vision isn't strong enough to warrant the clarity you want—and need—to give it. I hope by now you're seeing your vision more clearly and would urge you to re-read this chapter and re-do these assignments if you're not.

All of the chapters in this book are useful. Otherwise, I wouldn't have written them. However, some build on others and others even require some to be achieved before they are fully operational. Clarity is one of those skills you must possess to add value to the rest.

You can have great communication skills, but without clarity how will you know who to communicate with? You can be the most creative person in the world but if you don't have a clear vision of what, exactly, it is you want to do, that creativity is mostly for your own enjoyment.

Vision is not a soft skill; clarity is not an option. You must have a clear sight of where you want to go if you are ever to really get there. Clarity is what enables you to make your network work for you. Remember, clarity is the precision you apply in your life. It's the difference between first and second place. It's the difference between good and great. And, it's the difference between your potential ability and your actual execution. It's what makes YOU a savvy S.K.I.R.T. ready to truly experience your best L.I.F.E.: *Living In Full Expectation*. In fact, the primary point of the S.K.I.R.T.S. in the Boardroom: Set No Limits Summit is to help you see your potential, find your passion, and live out your purpose. Clarity is key. As I always tell people, if you can *see your future* you can literally *be your future*.

So, can *you* see *your* future?

Set No Limits Reflection

Clarity is the ability to use the lens of precise vision to see your own future before you actually create it. But, like a mirage, if you don't put the effort in to fully create and implement your driving vision, it can disappear like a shimmering ghost, gone in the blink of an eye. Answer the following questions to help secure, once and for all, your overriding vision before we conclude our journey together.

I would like to accomplish the following goals to achieve my vision.

- ◆ _____
- ◆ _____
- ◆ _____
- ◆ _____
- ◆ _____
- ◆ _____

These specific goals will help give clarity and precision to my vision by:

- ◆ _____
- ◆ _____
- ◆ _____
- ◆ _____
- ◆ _____
- ◆ _____

I can assign myself the following tasks to achieve my vision.

- ◆ _____
- ◆ _____
- ◆ _____
- ◆ _____
- ◆ _____
- ◆ _____

To achieve my vision I will need to do the following.

- ◆ _____
- ◆ _____
- ◆ _____
- ◆ _____
- ◆ _____
- ◆ _____

Bonus Chapter

What's Next?

How to Work Your S.K.I.R.T.

Now that we've embarked upon phase one of this journey together, you might be thinking to yourself, what's next? Where do I go from here? The beauty of being a savvy S.K.I.R.T. is that the answer lies with you. You can go wherever you like. Hopefully, you now realize that you can go boldly where no man has gone before. You are entitled to greatness. I know that, but it is up to you to embrace it. Once you appreciate the fact that you are capable of living out your potential and having the career of your dreams, it's up to the world to get ready for you.

I sincerely hope that you enjoyed reading this book. After all, I wrote it with you in mind. My desire is that the principles outlined in each of the chapters will distinctively enhance your thinking, your actions, and ultimately your life. However, the words on each page of this book are merely seeds. Reading the book alone is not enough to make the principles grow and bear fruit in your life and your career. You must take clear and focused action to see results and advancement.

In Part One of the book, I focus on four internal investments: confidence (self-esteem), class (attitude), course (direction), and commitment (dedication). In Part Two, I focus on critical action steps: communication (connecting effectively), connections (networking), creativity (resourcefulness), and captivation (creating your personal brand). In Part Three, I ask you focus on two factors that are vital to extraordinary, outside-the-box success for women today: command (L.E.A.D.ership) and clarity (vision). Each chapter contains a wealth of information for you to apply in your everyday life.

The Set No Limits Reflection Exercises at the end of each chapter are designed to help you style your life for a lifestyle of success. So, take time for your personal development and complete the exercises. People often skip over these exercises, but I can tell you that women around the country are experiencing life-changing revelations and transformation by taking the time to go through each of these steps. Nothing is in this book by accident. Every word and every exercise was specifically designed to help you optimize your potential. In order to get somewhere you have never been, you are going to need to do something you have never done. These action exercises are imperative.

I also recommend re-reading this book from beginning to end at a slower pace the second time around. There are 10 chapters. On your second go-through, I suggest reading one chapter per month and focusing on developing that topical area of your life. For instance, in month five, you'd be focusing on communication and dedicating the entire month to enhancing your communication skills in each of the areas outlined in that chapter. I guarantee your life will never be the same. Retaining is a product of reviewing, repeating, and reflecting upon lessons learned.

Make sure to bookmark and regularly visit www.skirtsintheboard room.com. That will be my way of staying in touch with you. You will find extended bonus exercises only available online. You can sign-up for the newsletter and receive invaluable resources, business tips, career development insights, and more. You'll find a section called "S.K.I.R.T. Spotlights" where I feature the latest success secrets from wonder-women making waves in a big way. If you want your company or your success to be shared, or if you want to nominate an impressive S.K.I.R.T., just send us an email.

Last, I invite you to attend a S.K.I.R.T.S. in the Boardroom: Set No Limits Summit. The Summit will provide you with a chance to interactively experience each of the ten core S.K.I.R.T.S. principles via a series of intense workshops, seminars, and power-networking sessions. The Summit will take you to an entirely new level of growth and career success. You will leave the Summit with a new way of thinking, a new way of being, and ultimately a new way of succeeding. And, you will meet hundreds of like-minded women dedicated to developing their personal and professional potential.

As I mentioned at the beginning of the book, the word S.K.I.R.T.S. stands for *S*isterhood, *K*nowledge, *I*ntegrity, *R*espect, *T*enacity, and *S*ubstance. One of the greatest gifts you can give is Sisterhood. As women, we must support and develop each other. The men have the good ol' boys club. As women, we have to create and nurture our own network. In the spirit of Sisterhood, I urge you to tell at least 5 people about S.K.I.R.T.S. in the Boardroom, and to consider getting the book for at least 10 other women as a gift. Companies are using the book as a training tool for their diversity programs and leadership development initiatives for women. If you've achieved any measure of success, I ask you to share what you've learned with other women. In fact, you can go online at **www.skirtsintheboardroom.com** to share lessons you've learned in business and to share your success stories with other women, as well. I cannot wait to hear from you!

Recommended Resources

ME Unlimited Programs
Equipping the Motivated to L.I.V.E. Out Loud

S.K.I.R.T.S. in the Boardroom Seminar

S.K.I.R.T.S. in the Boardroom is designed to equip women with the strategies necessary to combine confidence and compassion, style and substance, and, of course, beauty and brains. A must-have for all women looking to maximize their professional potential, S.K.I.R.T.S. in the Boardroom offers refreshing and inspiring business advice that is savvy, sensible, straightforward, and long overdue!

Habitude™

Habitude™ is a nine-step proprietary peak performance module designed to help executives and professionals maximize potential. The Habitude formula combines principles of *attitude* and *habit*. The training module consists of three levels. Within each level are three phases of efficiency. The presentation teaches a revolutionary, systematic approach to advancing goals, communication effectiveness, leadership, interpersonal connectivity, and workforce productivity. Each of these learning objectives is key in establishing a corporation's position in the marketplace and maximizing business growth from the inside out.

Instant Impact: Communication and Presentation

The single most important attribute influencing success in life and business is communication. Communication is more than just the exchange of information. It is a multidimensional pipeline that connects ideas, cultivates understanding, and creates productivity. During this dynamic and highly engaging presentation, Marshawn shares the secrets to becoming a standout speaker via the "V's of Communication." Attendees will learn their personal communication style. She also equips the audience with practical illustrations, presentation tips, and performance enhancement strategies.

Corporate Diversity: Valuing Differences by Adopting Different Values

In an ever-changing multicultural economy, there is a dire need to ensure the retention and promotion of diverse employees. Changing the corporate face requires you to face the changes necessary to cultivate a climate of inclusion that goes well beyond hiring. This presentation covers marketing, product developments, community outreach, goal-setting, strategic department integration, mentoring, and overcoming inevitable obstacles as key diversity enhancement measures. Attendees learn about the Seven Strategic "Asset Factors" necessary to improve recruitment and retention.

Executive EDGE: How to Make Your Mark

Having the EDGE in corporate America is a product of leadership, skill, presentation, and relationships. Ideal for MBA students, executives, and working professionals, this presentation equips audiences with a proprietary 3-Tier Executive EDGE Strategy: (1) the Four Spheres of CONFIDENCE^{TM}, (2) the Three Vs of COMMUNICATION, and (3) the Three Business Keys to Being COMPETITIVE.

Leadership for Life^{TM}

Leadership is more than a word; it is a way of life. This interactive presentation teaches participants how to lead by studying the Seven Dimensions of the M.E. Unlimited L.E.A.D.ership Pyramid. The workshop covers leadership competencies—the traits that separate bosses from leaders, along with core competencies such as business acumen, communication, self-direction, interpersonal skills, client relationships, flexibility, professionalism, and goal-setting. Attendees learn about leadership power styles, decision-making strategies, nonverbal and verbal communication techniques, attitude, how to L.E.A.D. (Listen, Educate, Act, and Discern), and the Leadership for Life^{TM} Four-Step Process: Receive, Reflect, Relate, and Respond.

Speaking Programs

Attorney, entrepreneur, and branding agent Marshawn Evans has been called one of the most insightful experts on the art of peak performance. She travels the country speaking for conference, colleges, corporations, and churches. To learn more about her speaking programs, training sessions, and consulting services, or to have her appear live at your next event, please visit www.marshawnevans.com or email info@marshawnevans.com.

About the Author

As one of the nation's leading experts on the art of maximizing human potential, Entertainment Attorney Marshawn Evans is Founder of ME Unlimited (Marshawn Evans Unlimited), a corporate life-enrichment consulting firm focusing on peak performance, diversity, and women's empowerment (www.marshawnevans.com). She is also the architect of the S.K.I.R.T.S. in the Boardroom: Set No Limits Summit, an intensive empowerment series designed to equip women to maximize their professional potential.

Some of her most popular presentation topics include:

◆ Habitude^{TM}
◆ The Female Factor: Readiness, Recruitment & Retention
◆ Gender Differences in Leadership & Communication
◆ Executive EDGE: How to Make Your Mark
◆ Branding Y-O-U: Power & Principles of Personal Branding
◆ Women of Faith in the Marketplace
◆ Women in Sports, Media, and Marketing
◆ Diversity: Value Differences with Different Values

As a pioneering woman in the world of professional sports, Evans is Founder and President of EDGE 3M Sports & Entertainment, a brand management firm responsible for elevating the profile of elite entertainers and athletes in the NFL, NBA, WNBA, and Major League Baseball (www.edge3m.com). Marshawn is also launching a motivational clothing line geared toward women.

A former Miss District of Columbia and Miss America Top 5 Finalist, Evans was appointed as an International Ambassador to the Summit of Achievement in Dublin, Ireland, and has served as a spokesperson for the National Invest in Youth Campaign. A native Texan and a former Harry S. Truman Scholar, Marshawn finished her undergraduate studies magna cum laude at Texas Christian University and graduated Georgetown University Law Center, which she attended by obtaining over $200,000 in scholarships. She practiced law with one of Atlanta's most prestigious firms, and has been featured by *Glamour* magazine, *Upscale* magazine, *Monarch* magazine, *Jezebel* magazine, *USA Today*,

The Big Idea with Donny Deutsch, ABC, Fox News, and on NBC's *The Apprentice* with Donald Trump.

She has worked on televised advertising campaigns for Lamborghini, Dick's Sporting Goods, Star Wars: Episode III, Bally Total Fitness, Dairy Queen, Best Buy, and Outback Steakhouse.

Marshawn, who formerly practiced as a commercial litigator and employment lawyer with one of Atlanta's most prestigious law firms, is a mentor with the Coretta Scott King Young Women's Leadership Academy. She is also the Founder and Executive Producer of the Caring EDGE Awards held annually in Atlanta, Georgia, which recognizes the contributions of athletes and entertainers in the community. Marshawn believes in strengthening the esteem of women while erasing stereotypes, and commits her time and voice to make that happen. Visit her online at www.marshawnevans.com.